Elements
of
Financial
Analysis

Elements
of
Financial
Analysis

Sylvan D. Schwartzman
Hebrew Union College–Jewish Institute of Religion

Richard E. Ball
University of Cincinnati

D. VAN NOSTRAND COMPANY
NEW YORK   CINCINNATI   TORONTO   LONDON   MELBOURNE

To
Jeremy Mark, Micah Jacob,
and
Peter Xavier

D. Van Nostrand Company Regional Offices:
New York   Cincinnati

D. Van Nostrand Company International Offices:
London   Toronto   Melbourne

Copyright © 1977 by Litton Educational Publishing, Inc.

Library of Congress Catalog Card Number 76-47204
ISBN: 0-442-27468-8

Published by D. Van Nostrand Company
450 West 33rd Street, New York, N.Y. 10001

10 9 8 7 6 5 4 3 2 1

Preface

Over a number of years, many of our students in courses and seminars in finance have told us that they need a ready reference work that would easily clarify financial terms, tools, and techniques for the application of financial theory to the solution of problems in an academic or business environment. As teachers and researchers in business finance, we frequently lamented the basic formality or rigor of textbooks and the logistical problems of assigning scattered readings that sought to teach decision-making in diverse areas of finance.

Elements of Financial Anaylsis should be particularly valuable to students enrolled in those undergraduate and graduate courses in finance in which cases are used to bring theory into a practical setting and where the book's application to decision-making may, therefore, be most effective. To teach the application of financial theory and techniques, our book uses a hypothetical business firm. The material is presented in the context of a single case study of a hypothetical company involved in multiple financial situations requiring analysis. By organizing the presentation around this extended case study, we reinforce and clarify the subject matter. This approach is, we believe, unique in financial literature.

We acknowledge a deep sense of indebtedness to all the authors of numerous volumes and articles who have enriched the field of finance and who have contributed in countless ways to the authors' knowledge and interest in this dynamic area of study. Special appreciation goes to Professor Z. L. Melnyk, of the Department of Finance, University of Cincinnati, for his generous assistance and encouragement in developing this manuscript. To him also belongs full credit for constructing the Present Value Tables 5 and 6.

Finally, our warmest personal thanks are expressed to Glenn M. Handler, M.B.A., CPA, a close friend and former student, for his enthusiastic and critical contributions to this project. Our secretary, Mrs. James Walsh, deserves our highest compliments for her painstaking devotion to the preparation of a difficult typescript whose innumerable problems she successfully overcame with unusual calmness and skill.

Sylvan D. Schwartzman
Richard E. Ball

v

Contents

4. THE TIME-VALUE OF MONEY 23

5. INTEREST RATES, TRADE DISCOUNTS, AND BOND VALUES 36

6. TAXES, DEPRECIATION, AND BUY OR LEASE DECISIONS 44

1

The Basic Financial Documents

A CASE IN BRIEF: THE LMN CORPORATION

The LMN Corporation, a large Midwestern industrial firm, is in the process of deciding whether or not it should introduce a new line of merchandise. To be able to manufacture this particular product line, the company would have to spend a net amount of $25 million at the start to purchase the necessary equipment. Or, if it prefers, it can lease the equipment over a five-year period at a cost of $20 million a year. In addition, the project will necessitate other capital outlays, including those connected with the extra cash on hand that will be needed, larger inventories, and considerably increased accounts receivable. The company estimates that over a five-year period its total sales will increase by $200 million, with net benefits after taxes of nearly $8.5 million.

As an alternative to buying or leasing the equipment, the LMN Corporation could purchase a smaller firm, the RS Company, which already manufactures this product line. The common stock of the RS Company sells over-the-counter for $20 per share, with earnings per share of $2.00. It has $1/2$ million shares outstanding and pays an annual dividend of $.50 per share. From the sale of this product, which is its only line, the RS Company currently earns $1 million after taxes.

The situation just described raises many questions. Deciding which ones are vital and how to deal with them involves much consideration. Even more, the decision-making clearly calls for the understanding and use of appropriate techniques of financial analysis.

OBTAINING THE FUNDAMENTAL INFORMATION

Where does the decision-making process begin? Financial analysis usually starts with the examination of a company's three basic fiscal documents.

1

The first, most basic document that reveals the financial state of a firm is its *financial position statement*. It is often also known as the company's *balance sheet* because it presents the balance between the firm's assets and its liabilities, including the stockholders' equity, at a particular point in time, generally at the end of the fiscal year.

The second basic financial document is the company's *income statement*, which presents the gain or loss achieved during the firm's most recent period of operation. Hence, it is also known as the *profit and loss statement*.

A company's third major financial document is its *statement of the source and application of funds*. It is also called the *sources and uses of funds* and the *statement of changes in financial position*. This document shows the financial changes that have resulted from the operations of a company and reports the flow of all funds between two stated periods of time—generally the two most recent years. The statement of the source and application of funds thus will show the flow of the firm's cash as well as its *near-cash* (that is, the remaining liquid assets), which together constitute its flow of *working capital*. Our preferred term in this case, *funds flow*, includes the flow of all forms of capital that may have occurred in any of the firm's transactions, such as the purchase and sale of property, equipment, investments, and so on.

THE FINANCIAL POSITION STATEMENT, OR BALANCE SHEET

As previously noted, the financial position statement, or balance sheet, shows the financial condition of the firm in terms of the relationship between its total assets and liabilities. Naturally, unless qualified by accompanying footnotes—which should always be carefully read—the value placed upon each item is that which prevailed as of the end of the stated accounting period, customarily the close of the fiscal year. But let us remember that it is always possible that unanticipated but highly significant changes may have occurred since then.

Another qualification that we should keep in mind is that the determination of the value of any number of items among the company's fixed assets—such as its plant and equipment—involves certain somewhat arbitrary decisions and may therefore be open to question. For example, equipment is subject to varying amounts of depreciation and the replacement costs of these assets may well be considerably more than the values that appear on the books. Nevertheless, the financial position statement is a valuable document from which much basic information about the condition of a company may be extracted. Figure 1–1 is a two-year financial position statement, or balance sheet, for the LMN Corporation. By comparing both sets of figures we can recognize and evaluate the changes that have occurred over the two most recent years of the company's operation.

FIGURE 1-1

THE LMN CORPORATION
Financial Position Statement
Years Ending December 31, 1976 and 1975
(thousands of dollars)

ASSETS			
Current Assets*	1976	1975	Change
Cash on hand and in bank	$ 10,000	$ 8,000	+$ 2,000
Accounts receivable (net of esti-			
mated loss from bad debts)	35,500	32,000	+ 3,500
Inventories	30,000	27,000	+ 3,000
Prepaid expenses	3,500	3,200	+ 300
Short-term securities	2,900	2,100	+ 800
Total Current Assets	$ 81,900	$ 72,300	+$ 9,600
Other Assets			
Property, plant and equipment			
Gross	$133,200	$125,500	
Less depreciation (straight			
line)	31,500	28,700	
Net	$101,700	$ 96,800	+$ 4,900
Miscellaneous assets (including			
notes receivable)	3,700	3,200	+ 500
Total Assets	$187,300	$172,300	+$15,000

LIABILITIES			
Current Liabilities			
Accounts payable	$ 25,000	$ 27,000	−$ (2,000)
Accrued income tax	27,100	25,200	+ 1,900
Other accruals	8,900	7,800	+ 1,100
Current portion of long-term			
debt	1,000	1,200	− (200)
Total Current Liabilities	$ 62,000	$ 61,200	+$ 800
Long-term Liabilities			
Bonds (6%, due 1991)	$ 37,500	$ 39,000	−$ (1,500)
Stockholders' Equity (net worth)			
$5 Preferred stock ($100 par)			
(20,000 shares outstand-			
ing)	2,000	2,000	0
Common stock ($1.25 par) (4			
million shares outstanding,			
1976)	5,000	4,800	+ 200
Additional paid-in capital (sur-			
plus)	12,050	11,500	+ 550
Accumulated retained in-			
come	68,750	53,800	+ 14,950
Total Stockholders' Equity			
(Net Worth)	$ 87,800	$ 72,100	+$15,700
Total Liabilities and Stock-			
holders' Equity	$187,300	$172,300	+$15,000

THE INCOME, OR PROFIT AND LOSS, STATEMENT

The second fundamental source of information about a firm, we recall, is its income statement, also known as its profit and loss statement. This document shows the state of a company's financial development during a given period of time—usually a year—that has ended in a net gain or loss. In a real sense it also provides a good picture of the management's efficiency in its use of the firm's assets.

Figure 1–2 is the income statement of the LMN Corporation for its most recent two-year period of operation. By comparing the two sets of figures, we can observe and evaluate the changes that have taken place during this span of time.

FIGURE 1-2

THE LMN CORPORATION
Income Statement
Years Ending December 31, 1976 and 1975
(thousands of dollars)

	1976	1975	Change
Net sales	$340,150	$320,000	+$20,150
Cost of goods sold	205,000	197,000	+ 8,000
Gross Profit	$135,150	$123,000	+$12,150
Selling, general and administrative expenses	100,000	92,000	+ 8,000
Contributions to employee retirement fund	1,000	1,900	− (900)
Total Operating Expense	$101,000	$ 93,900	+$ 7,100
Total Operating Profit	$ 34,150	$ 29,100	+$ 5,050
Non-operating income	$ 500	$ 600	−$ (100)
Total Profit	$ 34,650	$ 29,700	+$ 4,950
Interest paid	2,250	2,340	− (90)
Net Earnings (Income) Before Taxes	$ 32,400	$ 27,360	+$ 5,040
Provision for income taxes	$ 15,550	$ 13,135	+$ 2,415
Net Earnings (Income) After Taxes	$ 16,850	$ 14,225	+$ 2,625
Less: Cash Dividends (Preferred: $100 and Common: $1,800)	1,900	1,730	+ 170
Income retained in business and transferred to accumulated retained income	$ 14,950	$ 12,495	+$ 2,455

THE STATEMENT OF THE SOURCE AND APPLICATION OF FUNDS

The third basic financial document is the statement of the source and application of funds, also known as sources and uses of funds and statement of changes in financial position. This document provides information about the changes that have occurred in the funds position of a firm between two periods of time, generally during the two most recent years. The statement of the source and application of funds reflects the financial trends that are operating within a company in three ways. In the first place, it shows the growth or decline of the principal resources, or "funds," of the firm. Secondly, it reveals the firm's situation in terms of its working capital or liquid assets. Lastly, it reflects the company's cash position. All three trends are clearly evident in a company's statement of the source and application of funds.

The key to analyzing this information is allocating items to their proper category as a "source" or an "application" of capital. In general, Table 1-1 is a useful guide for determining to which category various items listed in the financial position statement, the income statement, and the applicable ledgers of the firm belong. Note how, with the exception of "payment of dividends," each item in Table 1-1 is actually the reciprocal of the one listed in the opposing column. Thus, "income from operations" is a source of the firm's funds, whereas "losses from operations," in the opposing column, require that the firm must apply some of its capital to make them up and therefore represent an application of funds. Similarly, each of the remaining items, with the one exception noted, is the reciprocal of its counterpart in the opposing column.

TABLE 1-1.

SOURCE OF FUNDS	APPLICATION OF FUNDS
Income from operations	Losses from operations
Sale of fixed assets	Purchase of fixed assets
Sale of investments	Purchase of investments
Increase in long-term debt	Reduction of long-term debt
Increase of stock	Retirement of stock
Decrease in working capital	Increase in working capital
	Payment of dividends

From an accounting point of view, as Table 1-2 shows, we see that the application of funds appears on the debit side of the ledger, and the source of funds on the credit side.

TABLE 1-2.

DEBIT	CREDIT
Any increase in assets or any reduction of debt or stockholder's equity means an increase in the APPLICATION OF FUNDS	Any increase in liabilities or stockholders' equity or any reduction in assets means an increase in the SOURCE OF FUNDS

Figure 1-3 is the statement of the source and application of funds as it pertains to the two most recent years of the LMN Corporation. The following notations specify those records from which the information was obtained:

[1]From the firm's financial position statement
[2]From the firm's income statement
[3]From the appropriate ledgers maintained by the firm

FIGURE 1-3

THE LMN CORPORATION
Statement of the Source and Application of Funds
Years Ending December 31, 1976 and 1975
(thousands of dollars)

Source of Funds	1976	1975	Change
[2]Net income before tax	$34,150	$29,100	+ $5,050
[1]Depreciation*	31,500	28,700	+ 2,800
Total Funds from Operations	$65,650	$57,800	+$ 7,850
[3]Common stock issued	$ 1,200	$ 1,000	+ 200
[3]Disposition of property and equipment	10,500	10,600	− (100)
Other Sources of Funds	$11,700	$11,600	+$ 100
Total Sources of Funds	$77,350	$69,400	+$ 7,950
Application of Funds			
[2]Dividends	$ 1,900	$ 1,730	+$ 170
[3]Purchase of property and equipment	62,300	63,105	− (805)
[3]Decrease in long-term debt	4,200	2,500	+ 1,700
[3]Increase in miscellaneous assets (including notes receivable)	4,600	4,100	+ 500
[3]Increase in working capital (obtained from the final section, below)	4,350	(2,035)	+ 6,385
Total Application of Funds	$77,350	$69,400	+$ 7,950

*Outflows of funds involve only those outlays representing an expenditure of capital. Depreciation and amortization require no such outlay. They become, in effect, funds that are still retained by the firm. Hence, as shown here, they are added back to the company's source of funds category.

FIGURE 1-3 (continued)

THE LMN CORPORATION
Statement of the Source and Application of Funds
Years Ending December 31, 1976 and 1975
(thousands of dollars)

	1976	1975	Change
Increase (Decrease) in Working Capital			
[1]Cash on hand and in bank	$10,000	$ 8,000	+$ 2,000
[1]Accounts receivable (net of estimated loss from bad debts)	35,500	32,000	+ 3,500
[1]Inventories	30,000	27,000	+ 3,000
[1]Prepaid expenses	3,500	3,200	+ 300
[1]Short-term securities	2,900	2,100	+ 800
Increase in Current Assets	$81,900	$72,300	+$ 9,600
[1]Accounts payable	$25,000	$27,000	−$(2,000)
[1,2]Income tax, current and accrued	42,650	38,335	+ 4,315
[1]Other accruals	8,900	7,800	+ 1,100
[1]Current portion of long-term debt	1,000	1,200	− (200)
Increase in Current Liabilities	$77,550	$74,335	+$ 3,215
Increase (Decrease) in Working Capital	$ 4,350	$ (2,035)	+$ 6,385

2

The Method of Dealing With a Case—An Overview

THE FOUR MAIN STEPS IN HANDLING A CASE

Before dealing with any of the specific questions posed by the case of the LMN Corporation, we must consider the total situation. In fact, the study of any finance case requires that these four main steps be followed:

a. Identification of the key problems and related issues, both quantitative and qualitative.
b. Determination of which procedures will be needed to obtain the required data.
c. Analysis of the documents by use of these procedures.
d. Evaluation of the results, with the ultimate goal of recommending the most advantageous course of action.

KEY PROBLEMS AND RELATED ISSUES

Generally, the key problems and related issues in finance cases involve one or more of the following matters:

Capital budgeting, or the application of the company's funds and other resources to specific projects.

Cost of capital, or the percent of interest or the discount rate that the company must regard as its cost for the use of funds, and, alternatively, what the firm must earn on its investments in order to justify this cost.

Capital structure, or the make-up of the firm's total capital funds; that is, its long-term debt, preferred, and common stock.

Funds flow, or the effect of the firm's operations on its after-tax inflows and outflows of capital.

Management of cash and other current assets, or the effect of the firm's operations upon its supply of cash and other current assets.

Merger considerations, or the value of a company-to-be-acquired and the financial consequences of a merger for the acquired and acquiring companies.

Each of these subjects must in turn be examined from two points of view:

a.   What quantitive or computational results emerge when the appropriate analytical techniques are applied?

b.   What qualitive factors (that is, elements that cannot be reduced to figures) need to be taken into account?

AREAS FOR QUANTITATIVE ANALYSIS

There is a wide array of quantitative techniques for financial analysis. Among the best known are those designed to deal with the following:

Common-size measurement; that is, reducing all items in an income or financial position statement to percentages for purposes of comparison.

Ratios of financial significance; that is, finding significant relationships between two or more items within a financial position and/or income statement.

The effective interest rate; that is, ascertaining the true cost of interest on debt that is being charged by the lending agency.

Capital budgeting; that is, determining the desirability of particular projects that a firm may be considering.

Cost of capital; that is, developing the overall cost of a firm's long-term funds. This cost determines the discount rate to be used in capital-budgeting, mergers, the flow and commitment of funds, and other financial considerations.

The firm's capital structure; that is, determining the optimum composition of the sources of all of a company's long-term capital.

Funds flow; that is, ascertaining the firm's future need for funds by analyzing its current and pro forma, or anticipated, statement of the source and application of funds.

Management of current assets; that is, determining how the company can best handle its current assets in order to ensure a satisfactory cash flow and adequate working capital.

Concerns involving mergers; that is, establishing the price to be paid for a company-to-be acquired and determining the possible consequences of a merger to the common stockholders of both the acquired and the acquiring firms.

SOME IMPORTANT QUALITATIVE CONCERNS

In addition to the matters that can be dealt with quantitatively through the use of appropriate analytic techniques, there are various qualitative factors that can also be of great consequence to the firm. Among them are such concerns as:

a. The ethics and legality of a company's contemplated course of action.

b. The effect of a firm's decision upon the well-being of its customers, employees, the community, or society at large.

c. The potential response of the public.

d. The reactions of the company's stockholders.

e. The firm's timing in embarking upon a particular course of action.

f. The capacity of the firm to finance an undertaking.

g. The degree of risk to the future of the company.

h. The possibility that the current management will lose control of the company.

i. The appropriateness of the action to the strategy the company wishes to employ to achieve certain ends.

These and other qualitative decisions will obviously affect a company's plans. Certainly, a company is in a far better position to deal intelligently with the financial decisions it must make once all of the various quantitative and qualitative factors have been thoroughly explored.

PRELIMINARIES TO DEALING WITH THE CASE OF THE LMN CORPORATION

Let us now return to the beginning and review the case of the LMN Corporation. Observe how the case calls for the application of the four main steps in dealing with any finance case: Identifying the key problems and related issues; determining what analytical procedures should be performed; performing the necessary analyses; and evaluating the results. By following these four steps, the LMN Corporation will be able to decide whether it should introduce the new line, and if so, which particular approach—buying or leasing equipment, or purchasing the RS Company—seems most desirable.

Identifying the Key Problems and Related Issues

It is plain that, on the quantitative level, the LMN Corporation must grapple with three principal questions:

Should it introduce the new line of merchandise?

If so, should it buy or lease the equipment to produce it?

Or would it be more advantageous to purchase the RS Company, which already manufactures the product?

In making its decisions the LMN Corporation will have to consider:

(1) Its own relative financial condition, as well as the profitability and general efficiency of its operation.

(2) Capital budgeting, or what funds the firm might be required to apply to the production of the new line, whatever the approach.

(3) The cost of capital, or ascertaining what the company must earn on the investment of these funds at the current interest or discount rate. The firm will also have to determine what its actual discount rate or effective interest rate is.

(4) Capital structure, or how the company expects to finance the funds that may be needed for the new venture.

(5) The management of current assets, or how the LMN Corporation could provide sufficient current assets to satisfy an anticipated need for adequate cash and working capital.

(6) Funds flow, or the probable effect of introducing the new line on the firm's total after-tax inflows and outflows of funds.

(7) Merger considerations, or arriving at an acceptable price for the RS Company and estimating how the merger might affect the common stockholders of both concerns.

The LMN Corporation would no doubt also want to take the following qualitative factors into account: (1) To what extent should the firm risk taking on a new line? (2) How could it finance the capital needed for such an enterprise? (3) If it had to issue more common stock for this purpose, would its current management face the possible loss of control? (4) Would the new merchandise enhance the line of products already produced by the firm and contribute significantly to increased sales? (5) Are there any legal impediments to the project, such as possible charges of monopoly or restraint of trade? (6) And if the corporation does acquire the RS Company, how might their respective stockholders be expected to react?

Securing the Data

To some extent, many of the qualitative questions will be answered when the appropriate quantitative results are known. But there are some, such as possible legal difficulties, that can be decided only by careful, expert analysis of the pertinent facts. To secure the necessary quantitative data, the following procedures must be employed:

(1) Common-size analysis of the financial position and income statements of both the LMN Corporation and the RS Company must be performed in order to determine the relative financial condition and profitablity of each firm.

(2) Relevant financial ratios must be utilized to provide a clearer understanding of the operation and efficiency of both the RS Company and the LMN Corporation.

(3) The relative expense to the LMN Corporation of buying or of leasing the necessary equipment must be compared.

(4) If the LMN Corporation must borrow the funds to purchase the new equipment, the effective interest rates must be calculated.

(5) The costs of capital that the LMN Corporation may need for the introduction of the new line, or for the possible purchase of the RS Company, must be determined.

(6) The firm's capital structure must be reconsidered in order that it may decide how best to obtain the needed finances; that is, whether the company should increase its long-term debt or issue more common or preferred stock.

(7) The LMN Corporation's funds flow must be analyzed so that the firm can ascertain what the situation might be should it produce and market the new line.

(8) The LMN Corporation must decide how it might manage the anticipated need for current assets in order to ensure a satisfactory cash flow.

(9) An acceptable price for the RS Company must be arrived at if the LMN Corporation decides to purchase it.

(10)   Additional capital budgeting must be carried on should the firm contemplate the further expansion of its operations.

Summary

When the appropriate analyses have been performed, the LMN Corporation will have the necessary quantitative and much of the qualitative data it needs. This should provide it with a much clearer picture of the conditions it must meet if it is to introduce the new line of merchandise. Only then will the company be in a position to evaluate the alternatives and come to its decisions. Should it produce the new line? And if so, how precisely should it go about it? Whatever course of action the LMN Corporation adopts will be the end-result of a thorough process of financial analysis.

3

Common-Size Analysis and Other Measures of a Firm's Financial State

SOME IMPORTANT SUBJECTS FOR ANALYSIS

To secure the necessary quantitative information, we can make use of a variety of analytical procedures. In order to apply these procedures, it is necessary to understand not only the process by which the data may be obtained, but also precisely what information it is designed to produce. The following important subjects lend themselves to quantitative analysis:

a. The overall condition of a company.
b. The firm's financial operations: Its liquidity, indebtness, efficiency, and profitability.
c. The time-value of money.
d. Effective rates of interest.
e. The value and yield of a bond.
f. Significant tax factors.
g. Methods of depreciation.

COMMON-SIZE ANALYSIS OF THE INCOME STATEMENT

In assessing the condition of a company, we find it particularly helpful to use the process of common-size analysis. This involves reducing the various elements in a firm's income statement and financial position statement to comparable percentages. We employ common-size analysis to a company's income

FIGURE 3-1

THE LMN CORPORATION
Income Statement
Years Ending December 31, 1976 and 1975
(thousands of dollars)

| | 1976 | | 1975 | | Change |
	Amount	Percent	Amount	Percent	of %
Net sales	$340,150	100.0%	$320,000	100.0%	
Cost of goods	205,000	60.3%	197,000	61.6%	−1.3
Gross Profit	$135,150	39.7%	$123,000	38.4%	+1.3
Total operating expenses	101,000	29.7%	93,900	29.3%	+0.4
Total operating profit	$ 34,150	10.0%	$ 29,100	9.1%	+0.9
Net Income BI*	34,650	10.2%	29,700	9.3%	+0.9
Net Income BT*	32,400	9.5%	27,360	8.6%	+0.9
Net Income AT*	16,850	5.0%	14,225	4.4%	+0.6

*BI is Before Interest
BT is Before Tax
AT is After Tax

statement by reducing each of its elements to a percentage of the firm's total sales. Observe the relative size and importance of a number of items within the 1976 and 1975 income statements of the LMN Corporation (Figure 3-1) for illustration. Common-size analysis enables us to measure the relative results of each year's performance. So in Figure 3-1, for instance, we note that the firm's total income, both BT and AT, are proportionately larger in 1976 than in 1975.

COMMON-SIZE ANALYSIS OF THE BALANCE SHEET

Various items in the balance sheet, or financial position statement, may also be measured by common-size analysis. In this instance, each is reduced to a percentage of the firm's total assets. Common-size analysis of various features of the LMN Corporation's balance sheet provides the results shown in Figure 3-2. Note that, in a relative sense, the firm's cash on hand has moderately increased, while its long-term indebtedness has decreased significantly.

COMPARISON BY PERCENTAGE OF GROWTH OR DECLINE

Finally, using percentages for elements common to both the income and financial position statements will show the proportionate amount of growth or decline between one or more years. This can clearly be seen in Figure 3-3,

FIGURE 3-2

THE LMN CORPORATION
Financial Position Statement
Years Ending December 31, 1976 and 1975
(thousands of dollars)

| | 1976 | | 1975 | | Change |
	Amount	Percent	Amount	Percent	of %
Total assets	$187,300	100.0%	$172,300	100.0%	
Cash on hand	10,000	5.3%	8,000	4.6%	+0.7
Accounts receivable (net of estimated loss from bad debts)	35,500	19.0%	32,000	18.6%	+0.4
Inventories	30,000	16.0%	27,000	15.7%	+0.3
Property, plant, equipment (net of depreciation)	101,700	54.3%	96,800	56.2%	−1.9
Accounts payable	25,000	13.3%	27,000	15.7%	−2.4
Bonds	37,500	20.0%	39,000	22.6%	−2.6
Preferred stock	2,000	1.1%	2,000	1.2%	−0.1
Common stock	5,000 ⎫		4,800 ⎫		
Paid-in surplus	12,050 ⎬	45.8%	11,500 ⎬	40.7%	+5.1
Accumulated retained income	68,750 ⎭		53,800 ⎭		

which compares the LMN Corporation's finances over its most recent two-year period of operation. Each percentage is obtained by dividing the difference between the figures for the two years by the figure from the earlier year. Thus, with the following example of net sales we subtract $320,000 for 1975 from the

FIGURE 3-3

THE LMN CORPORATION
Selected Items from Income Statement
and Financial Position Statement
Years Ending December 31, 1976 and 1975
(thousands of dollars)

	1976 Amount	1975 Amount	% of Growth or (Decline)
Net sales	$340,150	$320,000	6.3
Total profit BT	32,400	27,360	18.4
Bonds	37,500	39,000	(3.8)
Total assets	187,300	172,300	8.7
Common stockholders' equity*	85,800	70,100	22.4

*Preferred stock, of course, is not included

$340,150 of 1976. The difference of $20,150 is then divided by the $320,000 of the earlier sales: $20,150/$320,000 = 6.3%. Observe how significantly the total profits BT and common stockholders' equity have increased. Over the same period, too, the firm's bond-indebtedness has moderately declined.

MEASUREMENT OF THE FIRM'S FINANCIAL OPERATIONS

Other relevant measures by which the financial operations of a firm may be gauged fall into four chief categories:

Measures of liquidity, which reveal how readily the assets of the firm can be converted into cash.

Measures of indebtedness, which reflect to what degree the firm relies on funds from its creditors.

Measures of efficiency, which indicate how effectively the firm's assets are being managed.

Measures of profitability, which disclose how profitable the firm's activities are.

As a preliminary estimate of the financial health of a firm, each of these measures has a distinct value.

MEASURES OF A FIRM'S LIQUIDITY*

There are three major means of measuring a firm's liquidity, or relative short-term solvency. Each measure must be interpreted according to the size of the particular company, the extent of its commitments, and the nature of its creditors.

Working Capital

Working capital is the firm's current assets minus its current liabilities, or $CA - CL$. It is sometimes also called *net current assets*. According to the LMN Corporation's financial position statement, the firm's working capital for 1976 is $19,900. This is arrived at by subtracting $62,000 (current liabilities) from $81,900 (current assets).

*For ease of computation all figures cited hereafter are in thousands of dollars.

The Current Ratio

The *current ratio* is the company's current assets divided by its current liabilities, or CA/CL. The current ratio for the LMN Corporation in 1976 is 1.32 times. This is obtained by dividing $81,900 (current assets) by $62,000 (current liabilities).

The Quick Ratio

The *quick ratio,* also called the *acid test,* is the firm's current assets minus its inventories, divided by its current liabilities, or (CA − Inventories)/CL.

The quick ratio for the LMN Corporation in 1976 is .84. This was determined by subtracting $30,000 (inventories) from $81,900 (current assets) and dividing the result, $51,900, by $62,000 (current liabilities).

MEASURES OF A FIRM'S INDEBTEDNESS

There are three principal ratios for measuring a firm's indebtedness. As such they also indicate the extent of leverage (the use of fixed-interest debt in place of common equity capital) and the margin of safety provided by total stockholders' equity, both preferred and common.

The term *leverage* derives from the fact that when the percentage cost of a firm's debt is less than its percentage of profit, the common stockholders possess a "lever" for increasing the earnings on each share of stock they hold.

The following are ratios for measuring the degree of a company's indebtedness:

Long-term debt divided by total capital funds, or

$$\frac{\text{Long-Term Debt}}{\text{Total Capital Funds}}$$

For the LMN Corporation in 1976, this ratio is 0.30. This was arrived at by dividing $37,500 (long-term debt in the form of bonds) by $125,300 (total capital funds consisting of bonds, preferred stock and common stockholders' equity). *Common stockholders' equity* represents the value of the common stock, additional paid-in capital, and accumulated retained income.

Long-term debt divided by stockholders' equity, or

$$\frac{\text{Long-Term Debt}}{\text{Stockholder's Equity}}$$

For the LMN Corporation in 1976, this ratio is .43, which was computed by dividing $37,500 (long-term debt comprising bonds) by $87,800 (stockholders' equity). *Stockholders' equity* consists of preferred stock and common stockholders' equity as described above.

Total debt divided by total assets, or

$$\frac{\text{Total Debt}}{\text{Total Assets}}$$

For the LMN Corporation in 1976, this ratio is .53. This figure was obtained by dividing $99,500 (total debt consisting of both current liabilities and long-term debt) by $187,300 (total assets).

MEASURES OF EFFECTIVENESS IN THE MANAGEMENT OF FUNDS

There are four principal ratios for measuring effectiveness in the management of funds: average collection period, percent of accounts payable to net sales, turnover of inventory in relation to sales, and turnover of inventory in relation to cost of goods sold.

Average Collection Period*

The average collection period refers to the number of days that accounts receivable are outstanding. This is obtained by dividing the average amount of accounts receivable by net sales, and then multiplying the result by 360, a convenient figure for the number of days in a year. In brief, the average collection period is expressed as (Accounts Receivable*/Net Sales) × 360.

The average collection period for the LMN Corporation in 1976 is 35.7 days. This is arrived at by dividing $33,750* (average accounts receivable) by $340,150 (net sales) = 9.9% (percentage of net sales). Multiplying this percentage by 360 (the convenient number of days in a year) produces the 35.7 days of the firm's average collection period.

The average amount for accounts receivable was obtained by adding together $35,500 (the ending 1976 accounts receivable) and $32,000 (the ending 1975 accounts receivable) and dividing the $67,500 by 2 to get $33,750*.

Percent of Accounts Payable to Net Sales

Percent of accounts payable to net sales, or

$$\frac{\text{Accounts Payable*}}{\text{Net Sales}}$$

---

*An asterisk with any of the items presented below indicates that it represents *average* amounts. So, figures connected with inventories, accounts payable and accounts receivable usually appear as averages of their beginning and ending amounts.

is 7.6% for the LMN Corporation in 1976, which is obtained by dividing $26,000* (average accounts payable) by $340,150 (net sales).

Turnover of Inventory

(1) **Turnover of inventory in relation to sales,** or Inventory*/Net Sales. In 1976 it is 8.4% of total sales for the LMN Corporation. This was arrived at by dividing $28,500* (average inventories) by $340,150 (net sales). The turnover may also be referred to as 11.9 times, which is obtained by dividing $340,150 (net sales) by $28,500* (net inventories).

(2) **Turnover of inventory in relation to cost of goods sold,** or Cost of Goods Sold/Inventory*. For the LMN Corporation in 1976 it is 7.2 times the amount of average inventories. The 7.2 was obtained by dividing $205,000 (cost of goods sold) by $28,000* (average inventories).

MEASURES OF PROFITABILITY

Profitability is measured (a) in terms of the investment that produces it, (b) in relation to the amount of sales, and (c) in connection with both investment and sales.

The Profitability of the Investment

There are three ratios that may be used to measure the profitability of the investment:

(1) **Profitability before interest and taxes (BIT) on total asset investment.** This ratio is determined by dividing the net earnings of the firm before interest and taxes (EBIT) by its total assets, or (EBIT/Total Assets). For the LMN Corporation in 1976, profitability BIT on total asset investment is 18.5%. This was arrived at by dividing $34,650 (EBIT) by $187,300 (total assets).

(2) **The rate of return on investment (ROI).** This ratio is determined by adding the net earnings of the firm after taxes to the tax-adjusted interest (NAT**) and dividing the result by the total assets, or NAT**/Total Assets. The twin asterisks used with NAT** indicate that tax-adjusted interest has been added back to the firm's earnings after taxes. The reason for this, briefly, is that for tax purposes interest is treated as an expense. Therefore, the amount that would otherwise have been paid to the government as taxes really represents a saving to the firm. Hence, this is counted as part of the firm's earnings.

Thus, in 1976 the LMN Corporation paid $2,250 in interest. At a 48% tax rate, the tax on this amount is $1,080, and it is this sum, which would otherwise be paid to the government, that is added back to the company's AT earnings of $16,850. The result is an NAT** of $17,930. So we find that the rate of return on investment (ROI) for the LMN Corporation for 1976 is 9.6%. This was calculated by dividing $17,930 (NAT**) by $187,300 (total assets).

(3) Rate of return on owners' investment (ROOI). This percentage is computed by adding the firm's earnings after taxes to the tax-adjusted interest (NAT**). Then this sum is divided by the total stockholders' investment (both preferred and common), which is the same as *net worth*. Briefly put, the ratio is

$$\frac{NAT^{**}}{\text{Total Stockholders' Investment (or Net Worth)}}$$

The LMN Corporation computes its 1976 rate of return on owners' investment (ROOI) as 20.4%. This is obtained by dividing $17,930 (NAT**) by $87,800 (total stockholders' investment, or net worth). ROOI is also commonly called ROIC, *rate of return on invested capital.*

Profitability of Sales

Three ratios are also used in conjunction with the second measure of profitability, the profitability of sales:

(1) Profitability before interest and taxes (BIT) on sales. This ratio is computed by dividing earnings before interest and taxes (EBIT) by net sales, or EBIT/Net Sales. For the year of 1976, the LMN Corporation calculates this ratio as 10.2%. This is obtained by dividing $34,650 (EBIT) by $340,150 (net sales).

(2) Profitability AT on sales. This percentage is arrived at by dividing earnings AT plus tax-adjusted interest added back (NAT**) by net sales, or NAT**/Net Sales. For the LMN Corporation in 1976, the profitability AT on sales is 5.3%. This result was obtained by dividing $17,930 (NAT**) by $340,150 (net sales).

(3) Percentage of gross margin. This percentage is calculated by subtracting the cost of goods sold from net sales and then dividing by net sales, or (Net Sales − Cost of Goods Sold)/Net Sales*. For the LMN Corporation in 1976, the percent of gross margin is 39.7%. This was determined by subtracting $205,000 (cost of goods sold) from $340,150 (net sales) and dividing the result, $135,150, by $340,150 (net sales).

*The percentage of gross margin may also be calculated as 1 − (Cost of Goods Sold/Net Sales). Alternatively, the percentage of cost of goods sold can be computed as 1 − (Gross Profit/Net Sales).

By utilizing this formula, the LMN Corporation can compute its percentage of gross margin for 1976 as follows:

$$1 - \frac{\$205{,}000 \text{ (cost of goods sold)}}{\$340{,}150 \text{ (net sales)}} = 1 - 60.3\%, \text{ or } 39.7\%.$$

The firm can also calculate its percentage of cost of goods sold using the ratio:

$$1 - \frac{\$135{,}150 \text{ (gross profit)}}{\$340{,}150 \text{ (net sales)}} = 1 - 39.7\%, \text{ or } 60.3\%.$$

The Rate of Return on Total Investment (ROI)

There is one final ratio, the rate of return on total investment (ROI), that we have yet to discuss. It combines profitability on sales and profitability on investment since it requires multiplying the percent of profitability AT on net sales, or NAT**/Net Sales, by the turnover of the total investment (which is the same as *total assets*), or Net Sales/Total Assets.

In simplified form, this ratio may be represented as:

(percent of profit-ability on net sales)		(turnover on investment)		(ROI)
$\dfrac{\text{NAT**}}{\text{Net Sales}}$	$\times$	$\dfrac{\text{Net Sales}}{\text{Total Assets}}$	$=$	$\dfrac{\text{NAT**}}{\text{Total Assets}}$

Note that both the percent of profit on sales and the turnover of the investment are responsible for the degree of profitability enjoyed by the firm. Therefore, as in the case of the LMN Corporation, a company's return on investment (ROI) in 1976 is really the result of its percent of profitability on net sales as well as the number of times its total assets (investment) are turned over. So in this case,

(percent of profit-ability on net sales)		(turnover of investment)		(ROI)
$\dfrac{\$17{,}930 \text{ (NAT**)}}{\$340{,}150 \text{ (sales)}}$	$\times$	$\dfrac{\$340{,}150 \text{ (sales)}}{\$187{,}300 \text{ (assets)}}$	$=$	$\dfrac{\$17{,}930 \text{ (NAT**)}}{\$187{,}300 \text{ (assets)}}$
5.27%	$\times$	1.82 times	$=$	9.6%

4

The Time-Value of Money

TIME AS A FACTOR IN THE VALUE OF MONEY

In financial analysis money has a particular time-value of its own that is completely independent of all monetary fluctuations, including inflation or deflation. This value is based upon when one receives or spends it. This factor, known as the *time-value of money*, must therefore be included in calculations of income and costs.

Growth Through Compounding

To determine the value of money, one takes into account both the time in which it is received or spent and the interest rate prevailing during that period. For example, $1 invested now at 6% per annum will be worth $1.06 a year from now and $1.124 two years from now because of the compounding of the interest. We customarily refer to such accumulation of compounded money as its *value*, or *amount*.

The Rule of 72

Because of the compounding of interest that occurs, we are able to use a handy rule of thumb, the so-called rule of 72, to approximate the number of years it will take for one's money to double when compounded annually at a particular interest rate. To obtain the answer, we divide 72 by the number associated with the interest rate. The result is the approximate number of years needed to double the invested principal. By applying the rule of 72, we see that it will take approximately 12 years to double one's money if it is invested at 6% interest compounded annually:

$$\frac{72 \text{ (rule)}}{6 \text{ (\%)}} = 12 \text{ (approximate number of years)}$$

The Present Value of Money

In contrast to the situation in which money is invested now and appreciates in value because compound interest is added, money that we do not receive until a year from now will be worth less because we have lost the corresponding compound interest during that year. (Or looking at it in another way, someone else who is currently holding that money is earning this interest that we are not receiving.) Therefore, at a prevailing interest rate of 6% per annum, the $1 we receive a year from now is currently worth only $.943. If received two years from now, it is currently worth only $.890. We customarily refer to the current worth of money that we receive or spend at some future time as its *present value*.

There are four main variations on the time-value of money:

(1)   The value or amount to which $1 adds up in the future if it is *invested today* at compound interest. This is known simply as *the amount of $1*.

(2)   The present value of $1 *to be received or spent in the future* (and which has therefore suffered the loss of compound interest all during this particular time-period). This is generally called *the present value of $1*.

(3)   The value or amount to which $1 *paid in per period starting now* adds up if it is invested at compound interest. The customary expression for this is *the amount of an annuity of $1*. [Note: The term "annuity" is used whenever a set amount of money is to be paid in or received at regular intervals.]

(4)   The present value of $1 to *be received or spent per period in the future* (and which has therefore suffered the loss of compound interest all during this particular time-period). This is normally called *the present value of an annuity of $1*.

THE AMOUNT OF $1

To calculate the amount of $1, or the value (amount) to which $1 adds up in the future if it is invested today at compound interest, we must compound a certain sum of money that we now possess by a particular percentage of interest over a specified number of periods of time. To see what occurs, observe Table 4-1, which shows the compounding that would occur if we were to invest $100 at compound interest at 6% over a three-year period.

TABLE 4-1

Year	Beginning Amount	×	Interest Rate	=	Amount of Interest	+	Beginning Amount	=	Ending Amount
1	$100		.06	=	$6		$100	=	$106
2	$106		.06	=	$6.36		$106	=	$112.36
3	$112.36		.06	=	$6.742		$112.36	=	$119.102

We could continue the compounding process demonstrated in Table 4-1 for an indefinite number of years. However, we can also summarize the procedure for expressing the facts as follows:

$$V = \$100 \times (1 + .06)^3$$
$$= \$100 \times (1.06)^3$$
$$= \$100 \times 1.1910$$
$$= \$119.10$$

In which:

$$V = \text{value in the future}$$
$$\$100 = \text{sum to be invested now}$$
$$1 = \text{original amount}$$
$$.06 = \text{interest rate}$$
$$3 = \text{number of years}$$

From this summary we derive the following general formulation for expressing the amount of $1:

$$V = S \times (1 + i)^n$$

In which:

$$V = \text{value in the future}$$
$$S = \text{sum to be invested now}$$
$$i = \text{interest rate}$$
$$n = \text{number of years}$$

After substituting the actual figures with our investment of $100 above in this formula, we arrive at the same result as found in Table 4-1.

We can simplify our calculations even further by utilizing special tables representing $(1 + i)^n$. *Table 1: The Amount of $1*, which begins on page 90, provides this information. If we turn to the interest column headed 6%, where n, the number of years, is 3, we find the figure 1.191. This we immediately recognize to be $(1 + i)^n$, as we determined by actual computation above. *Table 1* provides us with the factor for any particular interest rate (i) at a specified number of years (n). We then multiply the sum to be invested by this factor. With the use of *Table 1*, we merely apply this simplified formula:

$$V = S \times n]i$$

In which:

> V = value in the future
> S = sum to be invested now
> n = number of periods hence
> i = interest rate per period

Assume, for example, that the LMN Corporation invests $10,000 in five-year notes issued by another firm at 7% interest per annum. What is the accrued value of this investment when the notes come due? The known data is stated in terms of the formula as follows:

$$V (?) = \$10,000 \ (S) \times 5 \ (n) \ @ \ 7\% \ (i)$$

The factor to be used for $n]\,i$ may be found in *Table 1*, located under the 7% interest column at $n = 5$. The $10,000 (S) is now multiplied by the factor, 1.403, and the product is $14,030. This is what the notes will be worth to the LMN Corporation five years hence.

THE PRESENT VALUE OF $1

In dealing with the present value of $1, we are attempting to find how much less that $1 is worth today if we will not have it to invest at a certain rate of compound interest until a specified number of years hence. Suppose that three years hence we are to receive $100. Assuming that the money would have earned 6% interest over this period, we realize that the diminishing value of the sum is merely the reverse of the compounding that we did in the case of the amount of $1. The result, then, is merely the *reciprocal* of the previous process. So, if the amount of $1 is expressed as

$$V = S \times (1 + i)^n$$

In which:

> V = value in the future
> S = sum to be invested now
> i = interest rate
> n = number of years

and with $100 invested at 6% over three years it is

$$V = \$100 \times (1 + .06)^3$$
$$= \$100 \times 1.1910$$
$$= \$119.10$$

to reverse the process to ascertain what $100 would have been worth three years hence had it been compounded at 6% interest—that is, to ascertain its present value—we apply the reciprocal to the sum of that $100:

$$PV = S \times \frac{1}{(1 + i)^n}$$

In which:

$\quad PV$ = present value
$\quad\ S$ = sum to be received or spent sometime hence
$\quad\ i$ = interest rate
$\quad\ n$ = number of years

$$PV = \$100 \times \frac{1}{(1 + .06)^3}$$
$$= \$100 \times \frac{1}{1.1910}$$
$$= \$100 \times .840$$
$$= \$84.00$$

Such calculations, however, are unnecessary if we use *Table 2: The Present Value of $1*, which begins on page 95. There, under the interest rate of 6% where n, the number of years, is 3, we find the factor 0.840, which is identical to our own results. Hence, to ascertain the present value of any sum, we normally use *Table 2* with the following simplified formula:

$$PV = S \times n]i$$

In which:

$\quad PV$ = present value
$\quad\ S$ = sum to be received or spent sometime hence
$\quad\ n$ = number of periods hence
$\quad\ i$ = interest rate per period

So, if the LMN Corporation anticipates receiving $8,000 from the salvage of some of its machinery seven years hence and the current rate of interest is 6%, the facts are stated as follows:

$$PV = \$8,000 \times 7 @ 6\%$$

Table 2 indicates that the appropriate factor, under the 6% interest column at
n = 7, is .665. This is then multiplied by the $8,000 (S), and the present value
(PV) of the machinery to be salvaged is the product, $5,320.

THE AMOUNT OF AN ANNUITY OF $1

Annuities, we recall, involve calculations based upon the regular, periodic contribution or receipt of a set sum of money. In the case of the amount of
an annuity of $1, we want to determine how much $1 invested every year at the
same rate of compound interest will be worth at the end of a particular period of
years. Suppose, for example, that we pay in the sum of $100 annually for four
years at a compound interest rate of 6%. (We normally assume here that the
payment is made at the end of each year.*) Table 4-2 shows the results.

TABLE 4-2*

Year	Amount at End of Year	×	Interest Rate	=	Amount of Interest	+	Beginning Amount	=	Ending Amount	+	Next Annual Payment
1	$100		.06	=	$6		$100	=	$106		100
2	$206		.06	=	$12.36		$206	=	$218.36		100
3	$318.36		.06	=	$19.10		$318.36	=	$337.46		100
											(last amount invested)
4	$437.46 ($437.50 when rounded off)										

*If, instead, each payment had been made at the beginning of the year, we would simply
shift the addition of the final annuity payment back one year. Hence, if in this particular instance
the annual $100 payment had been made at the *start* of the year, the result at the *start* of the third
year (rather than the end) would have been $318.36 (the first two years of annuity payments with
compounded interest plus the $100 annuity payment paid at the beginning of the third year, or a
total of $318.36). This, however, is not the usual practice in computing the value of annuities.

Instead of engaging in the computations we employed in Table 4-2, we
can express the same facts mathematically in the following formulation and obtain precisely the same results:

$$V_a = S_a \times [(1 + i)^{n-1} + (1 + i)^{n-2} \cdots + (1 + i)^1 + 1*]$$

*The final 1 stands for the last amount invested.

In which:

V_a = value of annuity received or spent in the future
S_a = sum to be invested per period
i = interest rate
n = number of years

$$V_a = \$100 \times [(1 + .06)^{4-1} + (1 + .06)^{3-1} + (1 + .06)^{2-1} + 1]$$
$$= \$100 \times [(1.191) + (1.124) + (1.06) + 1]$$
$$= \$100 \times 4.375$$
$$= \$437.50$$

But *Table 3: The Amount of an Annuity of $1*, makes such calculations unnecessary. Under the interest column of 6%, where n, the number of years, is 4, we find 4.375, which we previously obtained by using the more complicated formula above. With such a table, then, we can utilize this simplified formula:

$$V_a = S_a \times n]i$$

In which:

V_a = value of annuity received or spent in the future
S_a = sum to be invested per period
n = number of periods involved
i = interest rate per period

The factor to be used for $n]i$ may be found in *Table 3*.

One example of the use of this formula is demonstrated by the following case involving the LMN Corporation: If the LMN Corporation decides to set up a sinking fund for the redemption nine years hence of some of its outstanding bonds, how much money would be available to the firm then, if it makes a yearly investment of $25,000, at an interest rate of 5%, beginning now? The answer is determined by inserting this information into the formula:

$$V_a = \$25,000 \times 9 \ @ \ 5\%$$

Table 3 gives us the appropriate factor, 11.027, located under the 5% interest column at $n = 9$. The factor is then multiplied by the $25,000 of the firm's annual contribution. The sum that will be available to the LMN Corporation nine years hence is thus $275,675.

THE PRESENT VALUE OF AN ANNUITY OF $1

In the case of the present value of an annuity of $1, we are again dealing with an annuity, but this time in connection with a present value. The present value of an annuity of $1 calculation seeks to determine what sum of money the

LMN Corporation must invest now, at annually compounded interest, in order to receive or spend annually a particular amount, commencing several years hence.

By using mathematics, we previously found that the present value of $1 is the reciprocal of the amount of $1. The present value of an annuity of $1, similarly, is simply the reciprocal of the amount of an annuity of $1. We recall that in the case of the amount of an annuity of $1 we used the mathematical expression:

$$V_a = S_a \times [(1 + i)^{n-1} + (1 + i)^{n-2} \cdots + (1 + i)^1 + 1]$$

In which:

V_a = value of annuity received or spent in the future
S_a = sum to be received or spent per period
i = interest rate
n = number of years

So, after we eliminate the final 1 (for the last amount invested)—something plainly not applicable in the case of present value considerations—we use the reciprocal. The present value of an annuity of $1 is therefore mathematically stated as:

$$PV_a = S_a \times \left[\frac{1}{(1 + i)^{n-1}} + \frac{1}{(1 + i)^{n-2}} \cdots \frac{1}{(1 + i)^1} \right]$$

In which:

PV_a = present value needed for an annuity
S_a = sum to be received or spent per period
i = interest rate
n = number of years

If we want to know, for example, what $300 distributed in payments of $100 annually over four years is currently worth if the money could be compounded at 6% interest, we would represent the facts as follows:

$$PV_a = \$100 \times \left[\frac{1}{(1 + .06)^{4-1}} + \frac{1}{(1 + .06)^{3-1}} + \frac{1}{(1 + .06)^{2-1}} \right]$$

$$= \$100 \times \left[\frac{1}{(1.191)} + \frac{1}{(1.124)} + \frac{1}{(1.06)} \right]$$

$$= \$100 \times (.840) + (.890) + (.943)$$

$$= \$100 \times 2.673$$

$$= \$267.30$$

Or, instead, we could utilize *Table 4: The Present Value of an Annuity of $1*, beginning on page 105, we find the same figure of 2.673 under the interest rate of

6% where n, the number of years, is 3. It is obviously much easier to use the results found in *Table 4* in the following, simplified formula:

$$PV_a = S_a \times n]i$$

In which:

PV_a = present value needed for an annuity
S_a = sum to be received or spent per period
n = number of periods the annuity is to be received
i = interest rate per period

Suppose that, in order to meet certain obligations, the LMN Corporation must pay $4,000 a year in interest throughout a twelve-year period. How much money must the company put out now, at 6% interest, to ensure that this sum will be available for such yearly payments? Inserting this information into the formula, we have:

$$PV_a = \$4,000 \times 12 \text{ @ } 6\%$$

Table 4 provides the figure for the $n]i$ factor in the 6% interest column at $n = 12$ years. The amount given there is 8.384. When this factor is multiplied by the $4,000 that is required annually, the product is $33,536. This amount is how much the LMN Corporation must pay in now in order to be able to disburse $4,000 a year for twelve years.

VARIATIONS IN CALCULATING THE PRESENT VALUE OF MONEY

The various simplified formulas that we have provided are useful in answering other questions as well. All that is involved in making them useful is mathematical transposition. Here are some examples that illustrate the point with the use of each formula:

a. Using the simplified formula for the amount of $1, or $V = S \times n]i$, we can determine the sum we must have now (S) in order to obtain a certain amount of money in the future (V). To do so we need only transpose the original formula to solve for S as follows:

$$S = \frac{V}{n]i}$$

Refer to *Table 1: The Amount of $1* for the factor $n]i$.

Let us suppose that the LMN Corporation wants to know what sum of money (S) it must invest now at an annual compound interest rate of 4% in order to obtain $10,000 six years hence. We turn to *Table 1*, where, under the 4%

column at $n = 6$, we find 1.265. Applying the data to the transposed formula above, we see that:

$$S = \frac{\$10,000}{1.265} = \$7,905.14$$

In a similar fashion, if we wish to find out what interest rate the LMN Corporation must receive if the firm is to receive a sum of $10,000 six years hence from an investment of $7,905.14 now, we merely transform the original formula mathematically to $n]i = V/S$. After substituting the known information we get:

$$6]i = \frac{\$10,000}{\$7,905.14} = 1.265$$

By checking *Table 1* across the various columns of interest rates at $n = 6$, we find 1.265 under the 4% column. The LMN Corporation's money, then, must earn 4% compound interest if the firm is to attain its objective.

b. By using the simplified formula for the present value of $1, or $PV = S \times n]i$, we can easily determine the worth of an item today from its estimated value some years hence. This is obtained by mathematically transposing the original formula to:

$$S = \frac{PV}{n]i}$$

Consult *Table 2: The Present Value of $1* for the factor.

Suppose that, because the LMN Corporation has just received an offer to sell, it wants to know what the salvage value today would be for a machine that would bring $5,000 four years from now at a discount (interest) rate of 7%. By turning to *Table 2* and checking the 7% column at $n = 4$, we find that the present value factor is .763. By inserting this figure into the transposed formula, we get:

$$S = \frac{\$5,000}{.763} = \$6,553.08$$

c. With the simplified formula for the amount of an annuity of $1, or $V_a = S_a \times n]i$, we can determine the sum that needs to be invested annually to provide a certain amount of money in the future. To get this information we mathematically transpose the formula:

$$S_a = \frac{V_a}{n]i}$$

Table 3: The Amount of an Annuity of $1 enables us to obtain the answer.

Suppose that the LMN Corporation wants to create a sinking fund of

$255,000 to be available 10 years from now. Therefore, it wants to know how much of a payment the company must make each year starting now if the funds are invested at 6% interest rate.

Table 3, at 6% interest and $n = 10$, gives us 13.181. By incorporating this into the transposed equation, we find that:

$$S_a = \frac{\$255,000}{13.181} = \$19,346.03$$

Thus, $19,346.03 is the amount the company must pay in each year starting now.

d. Similarly, the simplified formula for the present value of an annuity of $1, or $PV_a = S_a \times n]i$, is useful in more than one way. For example, by mathematically transposing the formula, we can compute the sum we must begin investing now in order to be able to receive or spend a certain amount of money at a particular point some years hence:

$$S_a = \frac{PV_a}{n]i}$$

Let us assume that five years from now the LMN Corporation expects to purchase a certain piece of machinery whose present worth is $18,000. It therefore wants to know what sum it must invest annually from now on in order to have the necessary funds then. Assume that the interest rate is 6% and turn to *Table 4: The Present Value of an Annuity of $1*. The table, under the interest column headed by 6%, where the number of years, n, equals 5, provides the factor, which is 4.212. By introducing this factor into the transposed formula, we get:

$$S_a = \frac{\$18,000}{4.212} = \$4,273.50$$

This, of course, is the annual sum the company needs to invest starting now.

WITH INTEREST PAID OTHER THAN ANNUALLY

On occasion, interest may be paid quarterly, semiannually, or even monthly rather than annually. Such changes can easily be accommodated within each of the simplified formulas by adjusting the $n]i$ factor accordingly. For example, if the interest rate of 9% is compounded semiannually, n (the number of periods involved) would have to reflect two periods per year rather than one, and the interest rate (i) for each period would be 9%/2, or 4½%. Thus the various tables would be read under the 4½% interest column, with two periods of payment called for during each year involved. The same principle is followed for interest that is paid quarterly or even monthly. In this latter case, n would be 12 periods per year and i would be 9%/12, or ¾%.

Thus, the amount of money that the LMN Corporation would obtain from an investment of $26,000 over four years at 6% interest compounded monthly would be calculated as follows:

$$V = S \times n]i$$

$$= \$26,000 \times 48 \ @ \ \frac{9\%}{12}$$

$$= \$26,000 \times 48 \ @ \ ¾\%$$

$$= \$26,000 \times 1.430$$

$$= \$37,206$$

WITH MONTHLY ANNUITIES

Naturally, the present value of money will also vary if regular annuity payments are made or received *monthly*. Here, however, special tables are needed; they are supplied as *Tables 5* and *6* of this book.

a. *Table 5: The Present Value of $1/12 to be Received Monthly for N Years* gives us the present value of $1 to be *received or spent each year on a monthly basis starting now*. The simplified formula used is essentially that given for the present value of an annuity of $1, with the single variation that a monthly, rather than annual, payment is involved.

$$PV_{am} = S_{am} \times n]i$$

In which:

PV_{am} = present value of an annuity received or spent monthly
S_{am} = sum provided annually on a monthly basis
n = number of yearly periods involved on a monthly basis
i = interest rate per period

Suppose that the LMN Corporation will now begin receiving patent royalties of $5,000 a year on a monthly basis for nine years. The company plans to invest these payments regularly at 6% annual interest. How much money, measured in terms of its present value, will the firm finally realize?

By applying the known data to the above formula and utilizing *Table 5*, we find that:

$$PV_{am} = \$5,000 \times 6.752 = \$33,760$$

b. If, on the other hand, we wish to know *the present value of annual sums to be received or spent monthly during some year in the future*, we use the same simplified formula but with a different set of figures for $n]i$. These may be found in *Table 6: The Present Value of $1/12 Received Monthly in Year N*, which starts on page 113.

Let us assume that the LMN Corporation wishes to establish a fund of $120,000 out of which it will augment pensions on a monthly basis, beginning 10 years from now. How much would the firm have to invest now, assuming it could get 7% interest per annum?

In *Table 6*, we find that the 7% interest column at 10 periods gives us the factor .498. After inserting the known data into the formula, we get:

$$PV_{am} = \$120,000 \times .498 = \$59,760$$

This is the amount the firm must invest now if it is to achieve its pension objectives.

Interest Rates, Trade Discounts and Bond Values

THE EFFECTIVE RATE OF INTEREST

In connection with present value calculations, we observed to what extent interest (and discount) rates play a part in financial analysis. But, as we observe here, interest rates are also directly associated with trade discounts that a firm may be given for early payment of its bills and with the price of bonds and the yields one receives.

Let us immediately recognize that there is often a difference between the declared, or *stated,* rate of interest that is cited and the real, or *effective,* rate that actually prevails. Although we may know the stated rate of interest, as in the case of a bond or bank loan, this is frequently not the effective rate. Such a situation will exist with:

a. *Bank interest (discount),* which deducts the interest on a loan in advance;

b. Bills offering a trade discount, which in effect represents the return of a certain rate of interest;

c. All instances of interest based on the payment of monthly or yearly installments; and

d. Situations in which the real yield and worth of a bond differ from its stated yield and par value.*

---

*In each instance that follows, the interest rates mentioned are before-tax. The after-tax rate is obtained by simply multiplying the BT interest rate times 1-minus-the-tax rate. (See also pages 44–45.)

CALCULATING BANK INTEREST

Unlike simple interest, *bank interest* is really a form of discounting since the interest on the loan has already been added to the amount borrowed and, therefore, the bank has already taken its discount in advance. Thus, if a borrower were to take out a loan of $1,000 for a year at an interest rate of 7% per annum, he or she would sign a note for $1,000. However, this note already incorporates the year's interest of $70, so that all the borrower actually receives is $930.

The effective rate of interest in our example is clearly more than the 7% stated. The bank interest, or effective rate, is actually 7.53%. This is calculated by merely transposing the following formula for determining the amount of simple interest.

$$i \text{ (amount of interest)} = S \text{ (sum borrowed)} \times i \text{ (rate)} \times t \text{ (time)}$$

To find the effective rate of interest, we insert the known data and transpose the formula.

$$\$70 \ (i) = \$930 \ (s) \times r \text{ (rate)} \times 1 \ (t)$$

$$r \text{ (rate)} = \frac{\$70 \ (i)}{\$930 \ (S)} \times 1 \ (t)$$

$$= .0753, \text{ or } 7.53\% \text{ (effective rate)}$$

COMPUTING TRADE DISCOUNTS

A *trade discount* is a special reduction offered to a customer on the condition that he or she pay a bill within a short period of time, considerably before it is actually due. In reality, a trade discount is simply an effective annual rate of interest by which the bill will be discounted. To determine the rate, we first calculate the amount of the discount the customer will receive. This sum is then divided by the net amount of the bill; that is, by the total amount minus the discount. The resulting figure is the rate of interest for the period involved. The effective *annual* rate, then, will simply be the rate of interest for that period, times the number of such periods in a year.

Let us suppose that the LMN Corporation has received a bill for $10,000 marked 2/10 *n*/30 or 2/10 net 30. This means that the company will receive a 2% discount if it pays the bill within 10 days. If, however, it pays its bill within 30 days, when it is actually due, the company will receive no discount. If it does not take the discount, the firm will lose 2% of $10,000, or $200, for retaining its money for the 20 extra days it can delay its payment. This is a loss of

$$\frac{\$200 \text{ (amount of discount)}}{\$10,000 - \$200} = \frac{\$200}{\$9,800} = .0204, \text{ or } 2.04\%.$$

Since 20 days is approximately $^1/_{18}$ of a year, the annual effective rate of interest of this trade discount to the LMN Corporation is $18 \times 2.04\%$, or 36.72%.

ASCERTAINING THE TRUE INTEREST ON INSTALLMENT PAYMENTS

There are several ways in which interest on installment purchases can be computed. Two of the more commonly used are: (a) the *Merchant's rule*, and (b) the *United States rule*.

The Merchant's Rule

The so-called Merchant's rule allows us to compute installment interest on the original debt and on each partial payment to the due date. Table 5-1 illustrates the calculation of the Merchant's interest of 6% on a loan of $1,000, to be paid over a year in four installments.

TABLE 5-1.

Original debt	$1,000.00	Third payment	$ 250.00
Interest for 1 year	60.00	Interest for 3 months	
Total amount due	$1,060.00	(¼ of 6% = 1.5%)	3.75
			$ 253.75
First payment	$ 250.00	Fourth payment	$ 250.00
Interest for 9 months		Plus previous	
(¾ of 6% = 4.5%)	11.25	payments	772.50
	$ 261.25	Total payments	$1,022.50
Second payment	$ 250.00	Total amount due	$1,060.00
Interest for 6 months		Total payments	$1,022.50
(½ of 6% = 3%)	7.50	Balance due with	
	$ 257.50	final payment	$ 37.50

By applying the following formula for determining the effective rate of interest (and ignoring present value calculations*), we find that the Merchant's interest in this case is 9.96%.

*To make use of present values we would simply convert the total amount due on the original date to its value one year hence. This would apply as well with the use of the United States rule that follows.

$$r = \frac{2 \times p \times B_{in}}{B \times (n + 1) - B_{in} \times (n - 1)}$$

$$= \frac{2\,(4) \times (\$1060 \times .015 \times 4)}{(\$1060 \times 5) - (\$1060 \times 0.15 \times 3)}$$

$$= \frac{(8) \times (\$63.60)}{(\$5300) - 3 \times (\$63.60)} = \frac{\$508.80}{\$5300 - \$190.80}$$

$$= \frac{\$508.80}{\$5109.20} = 9.96\%$$

In which:

r = annual effective rate of interest

p = number of payments in year

B_{in} = original balance × interest rate × number of periods

B = original balance

n = number of periods

The United States Rule

The second common method of computing installment interest, called the United States rule, calculates the interest on the unpaid remainder of the debt every time a payment is made. Let us demonstrate the use the United States rule with the same $1,000 loan used as an example above. We again assume an annual interest rate of 6% with a debt of $1,000 to be paid in quarterly installments over a single year. Table 5-2 shows the calculations we employ.

TABLE 5-2.

Original debt	$1,000.00
Interest for 3 months (1½%)	15.00
Amount due after 3 months	$1,015.00
First payment	250.00
Balance due	$ 765.00
Interest for 3 months	11.48
Amount due after 6 months	$ 776.48
Second payment	250.00
Balance due	$ 526.48
Interest for 3 months	7.90
Amount due after 9 months	$ 534.38
Third payment	250.00
Balance due	$ 284.38
Interest for 3 months	4.27
Amount due after 12 months	$ 288.65

By applying a slightly different formula than the one used with the Merchant's rule (and again ignoring present value calculations), we find that the effective rate of interest is 9.6%.

$$
\begin{aligned}
r &= \frac{2 \times p \times B_{in}}{B \times n + 1} \\
&= \frac{2\ (4) \times (\$1,000 \times .015 \times 4)}{(\$1,000 \times 5)} \\
&= \frac{8 \times (\$60)}{\$5,000} = \frac{\$480}{\$5,000} = 9.6\%
\end{aligned}
$$

In which:

r = annual effective rate of interest
p = number of payments in year
B_{in} = original balance × interest rate × number of periods
B = original balance
n = number of periods

DETERMINING THE ACTUAL INTEREST RATE PAID BY A BOND

To determine the effective interest rate of a bond, we compute the amount of interest paid each period, then add the discount we received in the purchase price of the bond or, conversely, we subtract the premium we paid for it. In either case, we pro-rate each expense according to the number of periods during which the bond will be paying interest. The pro-rated figure is then divided by the average of the sum of the bond's maturity value plus its purchase price. The effective rate of bond interest, thus, is represented by the following formula:

$$
\frac{\text{Interest Per Period} \quad \begin{matrix} + \text{ Discount Per Period} \\ \text{or} \\ - \text{ Premium Per Period} \end{matrix}}{\tfrac{1}{2}\ (\text{The Bond's Maturity Value} + \text{Its Purchase Price})}
$$

Assume that a $1,000 bond due in 15 years and paying 5% a year semi-annually (or 2½% per period) is purchased for $800. Then, utilizing the above formula, we can calculate the effective bond interest rate per period.

$$\frac{\$25 \text{ (semi-annual interest)} + \$6.67 \text{ (discount per period)*}}{\frac{1}{2} (\$1,000 + \$800)}$$

$$= \frac{\$31.67}{\$900}$$

= 3.5% (but note that this is only the percent of interest paid per period and there are two such periods a year)

Therefore, 2 (periods) × 3.5% = 7% (the effective interest rate)

THE WORTH OF A BOND BASED ON PRESENT VALUE CALCULATIONS

The worth of a bond is not based on its quality-rating (which is determined by its type and the credit of the agency issuing it) alone. The price one should pay for a bond is also established by computing the present values of both its principal and its interest per period. The sum of the present value of the bond's principal plus the present value of its interest per period is the bond's essential worth.

Suppose that a bond issued by the LMN Corporation matures in 15 years and pays a stated, or *coupon,* rate of 6% a year semiannually (3% per period.) But it is now possible to secure an 8% return on a similar bond of equal equality (or 4% per period). What, then, is the current worth of the LMN Corporation's bond?

The current worth of the LMN firm's bond is determined by making two present value calculations. The first is the present value of the bond's principal at maturity, 30 interest periods hence. The second is the present value of the 30 interest payments that the holder will receive. Clearly, the current worth of the LMN Corporation bond is the sum of both. In this case, as Table 5-3 indicates, the maximum that one should pay for the bond is $826.76.

---

*The discount or premium per period is determined by subtracting the bond's purchase price from its maturity value, then dividing the result by the number of interest payments each year, times the number of years remaining to the bond's maturity. So, in this instance, the discount per period of $6.67 was arrived at as follows:

$$\frac{\$1,000 \text{ (maturity value)} - \$800 \text{ (purchase price)}}{2 \text{ (interest payments annually)} \times 15 \text{ (years yet to maturity)}}$$

$$= \frac{\$200}{30} = \$6.67 \text{ (discount per period)}$$

TABLE 5-3.

	What the LMN Bond Provides	PV Information Sought	The PV Factor at 4% For 30 Periods	Net PV Amount
Principal at maturity	$1,000	The present value of $1 in 30 periods hence at 4% for each	.308	$308.00
Interest per period	$30 (3%) semi-annually	The present value of an annuity of $1 over 30 periods at 4% each	17.292	$518.76
Total maximum worth of the bond				$826.76

ESTIMATING A BOND'S YIELD TO MATURITY

Although there are extensive tables that provide precise information on the yield of a bond to the date of its maturity, the so-called yield formula provides a relatively simple means of approximating this information.

$$\frac{\text{Annual Stated Interest}\left(\begin{array}{c} + \text{ Discount} \\ - \text{ Premium} \end{array}\middle/ \text{Number of Years Yet to Maturity}\right)}{\frac{1}{2}\ (\text{Current Price} + \text{Par Value})}$$

In the example previously cited, the LMN Corporation has a bond with a par value of $1,000 that pays 6% annual interest. By applying the yield formula, we find that if the bond can be purchased for $826.76, its approximate yield to maturity is 7.83%.

$$\frac{\$60\ (\text{annual stated interest}) + (\$173.24\ [\text{discount}]/15\ [\text{years yet to maturity}])}{\frac{1}{2}\ (\$826.76\ [\text{current price}] + \$1,000\ [\text{par value}])}$$

$$= \frac{\$60 + \$11.549}{\$913.38}$$

$$= \frac{\$71.549}{\$913.38}$$

$$= 7.83\%\ (\text{approximate yield to maturity})$$

The answer we obtained by using the yield formula is only .17% off from the actual yield to maturity, which is 8%.

DETERMINING THE APPROXIMATE WORTH OF A BOND BY THE YIELD FORMULA

Instead of using present value calculations, as we did on page 41, we can also use the yield formula to more simply approximate what we should pay for a bond. In the case of the LMN Corporation bond of $1,000 par value paying 6% annual interest, we assumed that it was currently possible to purchase other bonds of comparable quality at an 8% interest rate. The yield formula establishes the approximate amount one should pay for the LMN Corporation bond as $813.08. This is only $13.68 less than the $826.76 we arrived at through the more complex present value calculations.

We begin with the knowledge that we can now obtain 8% interest paid semiannually instead of the 6% offered by the LMN Corporation's bond. Hence, the LMN Corporation's bond will be worth less than its face value and its purchase price will be appropriately discounted. So it will be represented by $1,000 − D (the discount rate). Since .08 is the desired interest rate, then D is:

$$.08 = \frac{\$60 \text{ (annual stated interest)} + D \text{ (discount)}/15 \text{ (years yet to maturity)}}{\frac{1}{2}[(\$1,000 - D) \text{ (current price)} + \$1,000 \text{ (par value)}]}$$

$$.08 = \frac{\$60 + \frac{1}{15}D}{\frac{1}{2}[(\$1,000 - D) + \$1,000]} = \frac{\$60 + .067D}{.5[(\$1,000 - D) + \$1,000]}$$

$$.08 = \frac{\$60 + .067D}{.5D + \$1.000}$$

$$.08 \,(-.5D + \$1,000) = \$60 + .067D$$

$$-.04D + \$80 = \$60 + .067D$$

$$.04D + .067D = \$20$$

$$.107D = \$20$$

$$D = \$186.92 \text{ (discount)}$$

Therefore, the approximate worth of the LMN Corporation's bond is $1,000 (par value) − $186.92 (discount), or $813.08.

Taxes, Depreciation, and Buy or Lease Decisions

DEALING WITH TAXES

Taxes paid to the federal government play an increasingly important role in the financial operations of a corporation. Not only do they directly affect the firm's income and its financial position statement, but they also are vital considerations in such matters as the cost of debt and the determination of the company's capital structure. Some treatment of the subject of taxes, then, is indispensible to financial analysis and one should be familiar with the following concepts, which will be dealt with in this chapter.

a. Tax shield

b. Tax related

c. After-tax costs

d. Determining before-tax costs

"TAX SHIELD" AND "TAX RELATED"

As we know, many of a corporation's expenditures are immediately deductible from its income as expenses, and hence may be deducted from its tax liability. Among these are the cost of interest payments, rent, and the like. The taxes that the company would otherwise have had to pay on the income from which these expenses were covered is customarily called the *tax shield*. In effect, these sums represent savings to the firm because it has not had to pay federal taxes on the income used to defray such costs.

The actual cost to the company of such tax-deductible items as interest payments and rent is the total expense multiplied by 1-minus-the-tax rate $(1 - t)$. This is called the *tax related* cost because had the full expense been taxable, no reduction in the costs to the firm would have occurred. Thus, with a t (tax rate) of 48% in effect for the LMN Corporation, the tax shield for its $2,250 interest payment in 1976—that is, the saving from the reduction of its income because of the deductibility of the item as an expense—is .48 × $2,250 = $1,080. The tax related, or effective, cost to the firm after the saving of the tax shield is $1 - 48\%$, or .52 × $2,250 = $1,170.

AFTER-TAX AND BEFORE-TAX COSTS

When after-tax costs (AT) of an expense such as interest or rent are considered, it is the tax-related, or $(1 - t)$, cost that is really involved. Hence, the cost of the interest to the LMN Corporation in 1976 is not the $2,250 the firm has actually paid. Rather, it is simply the tax related cost of $1,170, or $(1 - 48\%) \times \$2,250$.

It is frequently necessary to know the before-tax cost of some expenses for which only the amount of after-tax cost is given. This is quickly ascertained by dividing the AT amount by $(1 - t)$. In the case of the interest paid by the LMN Corporation in 1976, if we were given only the AT cost of $1,170, we could still determine the BT amount of the payment as follows:

$$\frac{\$1,170 \text{ (the AT amount)}}{(1 - t)} = \frac{\$1,170}{.52} = \$2,250$$

On items that are not considered expenses to the firm and hence are not tax-deductible—the repayment of the principal of a loan, as distinguished from interest payments, for example—the after-tax cost will be the amount itself. So, in the case of the repayment of $1,500 in 1976 toward the reduction of the LMN Corporation's long-term debt, the full AT cost to the firm is the $1,500 (the after-tax cost), which requires earnings BT of $2,885. This is arrived at by dividing $1,500 by $(1 - .52)$, the tax rate.

THREE WIDELY-USED METHODS OF DEPRECIATION

Depreciation is the annual computation, for tax and accounting purposes, of the estimated decrease in the value of a long-lived asset, usually less any salvage value. It may be arrived at by a number of different methods. The three most widely used are:

a.   The straight-line method
b.   The double-declining-balance method
c.   The sum-of-the-years'-digits method

The last two are called accelerated methods because they offer greater immediate tax and cash flow benefits than the others. In this respect, they are invariably superior to the straight line method.

To be thoroughly accurate, depreciation should incorporate present values since the current worth of the various amounts of depreciation will depend upon the time elapsed and the estimated discount rate.

The Straight-Line Method*

Straight-line depreciation unquestionably involves less complicated calculations than do the other methods. To compute straight-line depreciation, subtract the estimated salvage value, if appropriate, from the cost of the asset, and divide the result by the number of years of the asset's useful life.

$$\frac{\text{Cost} - \text{Salvage Value}}{\text{Number of Years of Useful Life}}$$

TABLE 6-1.†

Year	Amount of Depreciation	PV Factor [Table 2]	PV of the Depreciation
1	$1,000	.926	$ 926
2	1,000	.857	857
3	1,000	.794	794
4	1,000	.735	735
5	1,000	.681	681
Aggregate	$5,000	3.993 [Table 4]	$3,993

*The figures assume a discount rate of 8% over a period of five years.

†Because of its simplicity, the straight-line method is utilized throughout this volume.

Suppose that the LMN Corporation has a production machine that cost $6,000. The machine has an estimated useful life of five years, after which it can be resold for $1,000. The annual straight-line depreciation is calculated as follows:

$$\frac{\$6,000 \text{ (cost)} - \$1,000 \text{ (salvage value)}}{5 \text{ (years of useful life)}} = \$1,000$$

As Table 6-1 shows, the present value calculations in this example use the present value factor found in *Table 2: The Present Value of $1*. The aggregate depreciation over the entire five years is nothing more than an annuity and therefore requires the use of the appropriate factor in *Table 4: The Present Value of an Annuity of $1*. Observe that the results are exactly the same.

The Double-Declining-Balance Method

One of the accelerated methods of calculating depreciation earlier in the life of an asset is the *double-declining-balance method*. This method uses an annual depreciation rate that is a constant percentage: the percentage is twice the reciprocal of the estimated useful life of the asset being depreciated. It is this that gives the method its usual name of double-declining-balance. Note that the usual salvage value is not considered with this method.

$$2\left(\frac{1}{\text{Estimated Useful Life}}\right) \times \text{(Balance of cost remaining to be depreciated)}$$

So, in depreciating the same $6,000 machine owned by the LMN Corporation by the double-declining-balance method, we multiply the reciprocal of the estimated life of the machine by two. For the first year the depreciation is:

$$2 \, (^1/_5) \times \$6,000 = 40\% \text{ of } \$6,000 = \$2,400$$

For the second year,

$$2 \, (^1/_5) \times (\$6,000 - \$2,400) \text{ (balance remaining to be depreciated)}$$
$$= 40\% \text{ of } \$3,600 = \$1,440$$

For the third year,

$$2 \, (^1/_5) \times (\$6,000 - \$3,840) \text{ (balance remaining to be depreciated)}$$
$$= 40\% \text{ of } \$2,160 = \$864$$

The $1,296 balance that remains can be depreciated by similarly applying the same 40% over the final two years. Or, in this instance, because of the relatively small sum remaining, the company can switch to straight-line depreciation after the third year in order to even out the amount of depreciation over the final two years. Table 6-2 shows the computation of the depreciation of the LMN Corporation's machine over the entire five-year period based on the double-declining-balance method. Again, an 8% discount rate is assumed.

TABLE 6-2.

End of Year	Unde-preciated Balance	Depreciation (40% of Unde-preciated Balance)	PV Factor [Table 2]	PV of the Depreciation
0	$6,000			
1	3,600	$2,400	.926	$2,222.40
2	2,160	1,440	.857	1,234.08
3	1,296	864	.794	686.02
4	777.60 [or 648]*	518.40 [or 648]*	.735	381.02 [441.29]*
5	0	777.60 [or 648]*	.681	529.55 [441.29]*
Aggregate		$6,000 [$6,000]*		$5,053.07 [$5,025.08]*

*If the switch is made here to the straight-line method

To simplify the present value calculations, use *Table 7: The Present Value of the Depreciation of $1 Utilizing the Double-Declining-Balance Method,* which provides a close approximation of the aggregate sum of the depreciation's worth. For the example of the LMN Corporation's machine, *Table 7* shows a present value factor of .843. When multiplied by the $6,000 that is being depreciated by the double-declining-balance method, the result is $5,058. The difference from our previous calculations is only approximately $5; it is $33 when we switch to the straight-line method. Note the difference between the present value of the depreciation obtained by this accerlated method (around $5,053) as compared to that obtained by the straight-line method ($3,993).

The Sum-of-the-Years'-Digits Method

Another means of accelerating the earlier years' depreciation is to employ *the sum-of-the-years'-digits method,* which uses a constant rate of decreasing depreciation each year. It is computed by multiplying the cost, minus the salvage value, by the remaining number of years of depreciation divided by the sum of the digits in the total number of years in the asset's useful life. Depreciation is computed with the sum-of-the-years'-digits method as follows:

$$(\text{Cost} - \text{Salvage Value}) \times \frac{\text{Number of Years of Depreciation Remaining}}{\text{Sum of Total Digits of the Asset's Useful Life}}$$

In using this formulation, we calculate the first year's depreciation of the $6,000 machine owned by the LMN Corporation as follows:

$$(\$6,000 - \$1,000) \times \frac{5}{5 + 4 + 3 + 2 + 1}$$

$$= \frac{5}{15} \times \$5,000 = \$1,666.67$$

For the second year the depreciation would be:

$$^4/_{15} \times \$5,000 = \$1,333.33$$

And so on, until in the final year the depreciation is:

$$^1/_{15} \times \$5,000 = \$333.33$$

Table 6-3 shows a complete computation of depreciation, based on the sum-of-the-years'-digits method. It also shows the present value of the depreciation. Present value calculations for use with the sum-of-the-year's-digits method when the salvage value is less than 10%, are provided in *Table 8: The Present Value of the Depreciation of $1 Utilizing the Sum-of-the-Years'-Digits Method*. In our example, using a discount rate of 8% over the five-year period, the present value factor is .839. When multiplied by the $5,000 being depreciated, the result is $4,195.00. The actual amount calculated above from *Table 2: The Present Value of $1*, was $4,197.00. The difference, as we see, is quite small.

TABLE 6-3.

End of Year	Fraction: Years Remaining of Sum of Years	Multiplied by $5,000	PV Factor [Table 2]	PV of the Depreciation
1	$^5/_{15}$	$1,666.67	.926	$1,543.34
2	$^4/_{15}$	1,333.33	.857	1,142.66
3	$^3/_{15}$	1,000.00	.794	794.00
4	$^2/_{15}$	666.67	.735	490.00
5	$^1/_{15}$	333.33	.681	227.00
Aggregate	$^{15}/_{15}$	$5,000.00		$4,197.00

Table 6-4 is a comparison of the results of calculating the depreciation of the same $6,000 machine of the LMN Corporation with a salvage value of $1,000 by the three different methods, disregarding present value calculations. As Table 6-4 demonstrates, the second method, double-declining-balance, offers the largest early amount of depreciation in this case, and therefore the greatest tax-saving, particularly when present values are considered. This may not always be so. Although the two accelerated methods of depreciation obviously have more advantages to the firm, which is best must be individually determined. By using *Tables 7* and *8*, we can determine which offers the highest present value total and hence which method is most advantageous to the company.

TABLE 6-4.

End of Year	(a) Straight-Line	(b) Double-Declining-Balance (no salvage value)	(c) Sum-of-the-Years'-Digits
1	$1,000	$2,400	$1,666.67
2	1,000	1,440	1,333.33
3	1,000	864	1,000.00
4	1,000	518.40 [648]*	666.67
5	1,000	777.60 [648]*	333.33
Aggregate	$5,000	$6,000	$5,000

*If the switch is made here to the straight-line method

TO BUY OR LEASE*

Principal Factors in Making the Decision

Taxes and depreciation are involved, of course, when it comes to the firm's decision whether to buy or lease various long-term assets, such as plant, property, and equipment. If, on the one hand, the firm buys, it will inevitably have to make use of some method of depreciation. This, in turn, will affect its tax liability. On the other hand, the decision to lease long-term assets will eliminate the element of depreciation, but the expense of renting the equipment will now affect the company's tax liability in a considerably different way. There are numerous other quantitative considerations as well. Among them are the cost and availability of funds needed for purchasing a long-term asset and the cash inflows required to cover rental charges or payments on the purchase. But ultimately the overriding quantitative factor is the difference in the relative costs of buying and leasing.

Certain qualitative factors are likewise relevant to the firm's decision. Among them are such questions as how quickly purchased equipment will become obsolescent, how anxious the management is to avoid some of the maintenance responsibilities of property ownership, and how the company looks upon the financial risks growing out of the terms for purchasing or leasing such assets. Any of these considerations may contribute to the decision to buy or lease. Still, in most instances the major determinant will be the difference in actual costs.

---

*Essentially the same questions and answers are involved in a "make or buy" decision, when the firm determines whether to purchase necessary parts or supplies from others or to manufacture them itself.

Determining the Difference in Costs

In the case presented at the beginning of this book, the LMN Corporation faced a decision about introducing a new line of merchandise. Associated with this decision was another: whether to purchase the necessary manufacturing equipment at a net cost of $25 million at the outset, or lease it at an annual rental expense of $20 million over a period of five years and, therefore, a total cost of $100 million.

The real difference in costs cannot be determined simply on the basis of these figures alone. The costs must be refined by computing their present values, as well as considering the consequences in terms of both taxes and depreciation. Moreover, in the event that the decision is to purchase the equipment, the company certainly cannot ignore the costs connected with borrowing funds for this purpose. What, then, is the difference in costs for the LMN Corporation between buying or leasing the equipment it needs?

First the cost of buying: we find that the company must pay 8% interest on the money it will have to borrow.† Here, though we recognize that the company's usual tax rate is 52%, for ease of computation we shall assume a tax rate of 50% throughout. (The difference in results is really not of great significance.) The computations in Table 6-5 show the cost of buying. Based on present value

TABLE 6-5.

Year	Initial Outlay (millions)	Cost of Interest on $25 Million at 8% (with annual repayment of 1/5 of principal) BT (000's)	AT [1 −50%] (000's)	Cost of Funds: Interest & Principal (millions)	Net Depreciation BT Straight-Line Less Salvage* (millions)	AT [50%] (millions)	Total Outlay NAT: [Costs Less Tax Saving on Depreciation] (millions)	PV Factor at 4%** [Table 2]	Net Present Value (millions)
0	$25						$25.00		$25.00
1		$2000	$1000	$6.0	$4	$2	$ 4.0	.962	$ 3.85
2		$1600	$ 800	$5.8	$4	$2	$ 3.8	.925	$ 3.52
3		$1200	$ 600	$5.6	$4	$2	$ 3.6	.889	$ 3.20
4		$ 800	$ 400	$5.4	$4	$2	$ 3.4	.855	$ 2.91
5		$ 400	$ 200	$5.2	$4	$2	($ 1.8) [after salvage of $5]	.822	($ 1.49)
Total net PV of outlay									$36.99

*Salvage value is estimated at $5 million.

**Since interest is tax-deductible and we are using a 50% tax-rate, the cost to the firm is only 50% AT. Therefore, the interest rate of 8% becomes a cost of 4% AT, or (1 − 50%) × 8% = 4%.

---

†Even if the firm possesses the funds itself, it must certainly take into account the opportunity costs for the use of its money; i.e., the percentage of return that the company could receive

considerations, the total cost, including the cost of funds to the LMN Corporation, is $36.99 million.†

Now, what is the cost to the LMN Corporation if it leases the equipment over the same five-year period at an annual expense of $20 million? The calculations in Table 6-6 provide us with the answer.

TABLE 6-6.

Item	Details	Amount BT (millions)	Amount AT [1 − t = 50%] (millions)	PV Factor (at 4% for 5 years)*	Net Present Value (millions)
Annual payments on leased equipment	5 year lease at $20 million per year	$20	$10	$4.452 [Table 4]	$44.52
Total net PV of outlay					$44.52

*With net amounts after tax (NAT), the present value percentage is (1 − t) × the interest or discount rate.

A comparison of buying and leasing costs thus shows that if the LMN Corporation purchases the equipment the cost will be $36.99 million. If it leases the equipment, the expense will be $44.52 million. Therefore, without taking any other considerations into account, buying is cheaper than leasing by $7.53 million.

Since it stands to reason that the lessor expects to make a profit, we can normally anticipate greater costs with leasing than with buying. There are, however, circumstances when the opposite will be true, particularly when the lessor is able to purchase his equipment wholesale or at considerable discount. Still, we must remember, cost alone does not always determine the final decision. Actually, for a variety of other reasons, including such qualitative factors as the possible rapid obsolescence of equipment, the firm may even prefer to spend more money to rent rather than buy. The decision as to whether to buy or lease, therefore, can only be determined after thorough analysis of all the factors.

were it to lend the money to others or use it for projects that would produce additional revenue for itself.

†No consideration has been given here to certain other costs that might be incurred with buying or leasing, such as legal fees, bank charges, maintenance costs, and the like.

7

Capital Budgeting

THE NATURE OF CAPITAL BUDGETING

Capital budgeting refers to the process by which a firm determines where to apply its comparatively limited financial resources. Whether the company actually possesses these resources at the time or must obtain them from outside sources, it is involved in making capital budgeting decisions, usually by gauging the net cash flow AT to the company from the use of that capital.

Firms normally face four types of demand for capital budgeting:

a. To maintain or improve existing operations through the saving of costs or the improvement of a product.

b. To expand existing operations by producing and marketing new products or creating new facilities.

c. To introduce certain necessary though nonproductive improvements, such as measures to protect against fire or to comply with safety or environmental regulations.

d. To increase its program of research and development.

By ranking projects according to established criteria, a company can determine desirabilities and priorities. "Accept or reject" decisions will enable the company to select those projects that appear to be of greatest benefit, and in making them the company will certainly want to take into account significant qualitative and quantitative factors.

QUALITATIVE CONSIDERATIONS

Although we have repeatedly referred to the importance of quantitative concerns, as we have mentioned before, the firm must consider the potential impact of qualitative considerations with any project. Among the questions it must raise are:

a. The degree of risk to the firm that the project presents.

b. The likely length of the economic life of the project.

c. Possible adverse social consequences that could affect the firm's employees or the community, such as automation, pollution, the closing of a plant, and the like.

d. Potential strategic benefits to the company, such as occur when a project enables the company to compete more effectively or ensures the supply of certain parts for already existing products.

THE SUM NEEDED FOR AN INVESTMENT PROJECT

Because every project requires an immediate investment of funds, the firm must determine as quickly as possible:

a. The total amount of funds needed to finance the project, or, in essence, the application of funds.

b. How much of this amount the project itself will generate during the initial time-period, or its contribution to the source of funds and, within this, the firm's cash flow.

c. The balance (funds not generated by the project itself) needed to finance the total investment during the initial period, or the difference between the source and the application of funds.

d. How the firm will decide to finance that difference between the source and application of funds. How the firm ultimately finances that difference requires it to make decisions about its capital structure.

With the first three items, we are dealing essentially with the creation of a pro forma, or anticipated, statement of the source and application of funds for the first year of the project. (A quick review of the material on pages 5–7 will be helpful.)

A *pro forma statement of the need for funds* has been developed to take into account the basic elements in Figure 7-1.

FIGURE 7-1

PRO FORMA STATEMENT OF THE NEED FOR FUNDS
LMN CORPORATION
January 1, 1977

Estimated year's increase in sales as a result of the new project (initially based on the previous average percentage of growth in the firm's income; also see pages 56–61.

Estimated year's net income BT (based on the ratio, expressed as a percentage, of the firm's previous average income to average sales) [SOURCE]

Funds needed: Estimated increases in current assets (based on the ratio, expressed as a percentage, of the company's previous average current assets to average sales) [APPLICATION]

Estimated amount of total funds needed [APPLICATION]

    Less: Increase in current liabilities (based on the ratio of their previous average amount to sales) [SOURCE]

    Less: Retained income remaining from estimated net income BT listed above, less taxes (based on a percentage of the average amount to income AT) [SOURCE]

Total reduction from estimated amount of funds needed [SOURCE]

Estimated net total amount needed to finance the increase in sales (and hence the project) [Total APPLICATION less total SOURCE]

Assuming that the proposed project of the LMN Corporation will produce an estimated increase in sales of $20 million for the coming year, the amount needed to finance the project would be determined as shown in Figure 7-2.

FIGURE 7-2

PRO FORMA STATEMENT OF THE NEEDS FOR FUNDS
LMN CORPORATION
January 1, 1977
(thousands of dollars)

Estimated year's increase in sales due to the new project	$20,000
Estimated year's net income BT (based on 9.1%, the average percentage of prior operating profit to average sales)	1,820

FIGURE 7-2 (continued)

PRO FORMA STATEMENT OF THE NEED FOR FUNDS
LMN CORPORATION
January 1, 1977
(thousands of dollars)

Estimated funds needed:
  Increases in average of current assets based
    on:
    Necessary cash on hand (2.7% of average
      sales) $ 540
    Accounts receivable (10.2% of average
      sales)   2,040
    Inventories (8.6% of average sales)   1,720
    Net property, plant, equipment (30.1% of
      average sales)   6,020
Estimated total funds needed $10,320
  Less: Increase in current liabilities (18.7% of
    sales) $3,740
  Less: Retained income (from Income of
    $1,820 BT times .52, the AT amount
    = $946, less average cash dividend pay-
    ment of 11.7% [or $111] of average income
    AT = $835)   835
  Total reduction from estimated funds needed   4,575
Estimated net total amount needed to finance
  the increase in sales (and hence the project) $ 5,745

As Figure 7-2 indicates, the LMN Corporation will be required to make an investment of $5,745 more than the estimated return of the project during its first year.

PRINCIPAL WAYS OF DETERMINING A PROJECT'S NET RETURN

Qualitative considerations or the pro forma statement of the need for funds will often resolve the question of whether a company should undertake a new project. In addition to these considerations, however, the company is concerned with the total net financial return of the project. To determine the financial return, the firm may employ a variety of analytic procedures, of which the net present value method and the internal rate of return are the most frequently used.

The Payback Period

The *payback period* method is useful because it allows us to simply and quickly determine the numbers of years needed for a project to return its investment. Consequently, it does not employ the use of present value computations. In essence the payback period method measures the net investment involved in a project against its average annual cash return, so that the result provides the number of yearly cash inflows AT needed to equal the net outflow (investment). This is expressed by the formula:

$$\text{Payback Period} = \frac{\text{Net Investment}}{\text{Average Annual Cash Flow AT}}$$

Assume that the LMN Corporation is considering investing $48,700 in a project that could produce an average yearly cash inflow AT of $4,500. The payback period for the return of the investment will be 10.8 years, as seen from this calculation:

$$\text{Payback Period} = \frac{\$48,700 \text{ (net investment)}}{\$4,500 \text{ (average annual cash flow AT)}}$$

$$= 10.8 \text{ (years)}$$

The Accounting Rate of Return

Like the payback period, the *accounting rate of return* is a simple, fast method for arriving at the average annual rate of return, again ignoring present value considerations. Actually it is the reciprocal of the payback period and uses the formula:

$$\text{Accounting Rate of Return} = 1 / \frac{\text{Net Investment}}{\text{Average Annual Cash Flow AT}}$$

which by transposition becomes

$$\text{Accounting Rate of Return} = \frac{\text{Average Annual Cash Flow AT}}{\text{Net Investment}}$$

Again using the example of the LMN Corporation, which is considering a project with an annual cash inflow AT of $4,500 and an investment of $48,700, the accounting rate of return shows us that the annual return is 9.24%. This was arrived at as follows:

$$\text{Accounting Rate of Return} = \frac{\$4,500 \text{ (average annual cash flow AT)}}{\$48,700 \text{ (net investment)}}$$

$$= .0924, \text{ or } 9.24\% \text{ (annual return)}$$

Net Present Value

The most helpful means of determining the profitability of projects of intermediate length of duration is the *net present value method*. The results this method yields enable us to compare and rank various projects by using a *net present value index*. To use the net present value method, we first calculate the anticipated net cash outflows and inflows AT for each year of the project's estimated life. We then reduce the net cash inflows AT to their present values by multiplying each year's result by the appropriate present value factor. A comparison of the total PV of the cash outflows shows both the percentage of net PV of gain or loss and the net PV index.

$$(1) \quad \frac{\% \text{ of Net PV of}}{\text{Gain or Loss}} = \frac{\text{Total PV of the Cash Inflows AT}}{\text{Total PV of the Cash Outflows}}$$

$$(2) \quad \text{Net PV Index} = \frac{\text{Total PV of the Cash Inflows AT}}{\text{Total PV of the Cash Outflows}}$$

Observe the application of the net present value method to the following project of five-years' duration that is currently under consideration by the LMN Corporation. From the new project, the company expects sales of $40,000 in 1977, $50,000 in 1978, $55,000 in 1979, $35,000 in 1980, and $20,000 in 1981. Therefore, according to the calculations presented in Table 7-1, the LMN Corporation anticipates a net cash inflow AT of $6,420 in 1977, $8,500 in 1978, $11,840 in 1979, $6,120 in 1980, and $4,300 in 1981, including salvage. When reduced to present values at 8%, which is the percentage NAT that the LMN Corporation must earn on its investment, the total cash inflows AT add up to $33,462.

TABLE 7-1.
(thousands of dollars)

	YEAR 0 (1976)	1977	1978	1979	1980	1981
Estimated sales		$40,000	$50,000	$55,000	$35,000	$20,000
Less: Operating expenses (including depreciation)		31,500	37,500	38,000	29,000	17,500
Net earnings BT		$ 8,500	$12,500	$17,000	$ 6,000	$ 2,500
Net earnings AT		4,420	6,500	8,840	3,120	1,300
Add back non-cash expenses (including depreciation)		2,000	2,000	3,000	3,000	3,000
Plus estimated salvage						5,000

TABLE 7-1. **(continued)**
(thousands of dollars)

	YEAR 0 (1976)	1977	1978	1979	1980	1981
Net cash inflow AT		$ 6,420	$ 8,500	$11,840	$ 6,120	$ 9,300
Times the present value factor [*Table 2*]		.926	.857	.794	.735	.681
PV of cash inflows AT		$ 5,945	$ 7,285	$ 9,401	$ 4,498	$ 6,333
Net total PV of cash inflows AT						$33,462

The LMN Corporation must immediately invest $35,000 in equipment. However, from this sum it will be able to deduct: (1) the tax loss based on the depreciation still remaining on equipment to be replaced; and (2) the investment credit on the purchase of the new equipment, which together total $10,000. The company also estimates that at the end of the fifth year, when the project is terminated, the salvage value of the equipment will be about $5,000. (See Table 7-2.)

TABLE 7-2.
(thousands of dollars)

	YEAR 0 (1976)	1977	1978	1979	1980	1981
Investment	$35,000					
Less: Tax loss and investment credit	($10,000)					
Net outflows	$25,000					
Times the present value factor						
PV of cash outflows	$25,000					
Net total PV of cash outflows	$25,000					

As we see in Table 7-3, the net present value method indicates an ultimate gain AT from the project of $8,462.

TABLE 7-3.

Total PV of cash inflows AT	$33,462
Total PV of cash outflows	25,000
Net present value gain AT	+$ 8,462

The net present value index, which makes it possible to rank projects of different sizes or lengths of economic life, is obtained by dividing the total PV of cash inflows AT by the total PV of cash outflows. Thus, the figures in Table 7-3 compose the following net present value index (generally called the *profitability index*) of the project:

$$\frac{\$33,462 \text{ (total PV of cash inflows AT)}}{\$25,000 \text{ (total PV of cash outflows)}}$$

= A net PV index of 139 (or 39% higher than outflows)

Internal Rate of Return

The *internal rate of return*, also called the *yield on investment* approach, is useful in determining the profitability of a project. It differs from the net present value method in that it does not indicate the size of the investment; thus, the same rate of return may be obtained for projects involving investments of either $100,000 or $500,000. The internal rate of return approach also assumes a constant rate of return throughout for the reinvestment of the cash inflow. Thus, with projects of different lengths and of widely varying rates of inflows, this method may lead to certain distortions.

The internal rate of return method attempts to find the particular discount rate that will make the present value of the net cash outflows (or net investment) for a project equal to the present value of its net cash inflows AT. By applying the same net cash inflows AT and outflows that we used previously with the net present value method, we find that the internal rate of return method produces the results shown in Table 7-4 (cash inflows) and Table 7-5 (cash outflows).

To estimate the internal rate of return, we arbitrarily select discount rates of 18% and 19%, which, from the outset, seem to be likely boundaries for the PV factors for our answer. As Table 7-6 shows, the internal rate of return is, in this case, somewhat more than 19% but less than 20%. This makes it necessary to employ the process of *interpolation* between the 19% and 20% discount rates.

TABLE 7-4.
(thousands of dollars)

	YEAR 0 (1976)	1977	1978	1979	1980	1981	TOTALS
Net cash inflows AT		$6,420	$8,500	$11,840	$6,120	$9,300	
Times the PV factor at 19% [Table 2]		.840	.706	.593	.499	.419	
Net PV of cash inflows AT		$5,393	$6,001	$ 7,021	$3,054	$3,897	$25,366
Times the PV factor at 18% [Table 2]		.848	.718	.609	.516	.437	
Net PV of cash inflows AT		$5,444	$6,103	$ 7,211	$3,158	$4,064	$25,980

TABLE 7-5.
(thousands of dollars)

	YEAR 0 (1976)	1977	1978	1979	1980	1981	TOTALS
Net cash outflows	$25,000						
Times the PV factor at 19%	[1.000]						
Net PV of cash outflows	$25,000						
Times the PV factor at 18%	[1.000]						
Net PV of cash outflows	$25,000						$25,000

TABLE 7-6.
(thousands of dollars)

	Net PV of Cash Inflows	Net PV of Cash Outflows	Difference
Internal Rate of Return at 19%	$25,366	$25,000	+$366
Internal Rate of Return at 18%	$25,980	$25,000	+$980

THE PROCESS OF INTERPOLATION

If we want to obtain the *exact* figure for the internal rate of return in this example, we must employ the process of *interpolation*. Interpolation must be performed when, by using two contiguous percentage points (in this case 19% and 20%), we obtain figures for present values that lie somewhere between the two amounts.

Interpolation involves determining what fraction of a percent exists between the amount of the difference in the present value cash inflows AT and outflows that occur at the lower of the two percentage points, and the difference in the sums found for the present value cash inflows AT occurring at the two contiguous percentage points. More simply, the proportion we are seeking is:

$$\frac{\text{The Amount of the Difference in the PV Cash Inflows AT}}{\text{and Outflows at the Lower Percentage Point}}$$
$$\overline{\text{The Amount of the Difference in the PV Cash Inflows}}$$
$$\text{AT at the Two Contiguous Percentage Points}$$

To interpolate, we first find the difference between the PV of the cash inflows AT at 19% and the cash outflows at 19%. Looking again at Table 7-6, we note these results:

PV of cash inflows AT at 19%	$25,366
PV of cash outflows AT at 19%	25,000
Difference	+$ 366

Next, we calculate the difference between the PV of the cash inflows AT at 19% and at 20%.

PV of cash inflows AT at 19%	$25,366
PV of cash inflows AT at 20%	24,791
Difference	−$ 575

To determine what fraction of a percent we are seeking, we observe that the unknown rate lies between

$$\frac{\$366 \text{ (PV of cash inflows AT at 19\% } - \text{ PV of cash outflows at 19\%)}}{\$575 \text{ (PV of cash inflows AT at 19\% } - \text{ PV of cash inflows AT at 20\%)}}$$

When we compute the actual rate, we get 366/575 of 1%, which equals .64 of 1%, or .64%. Therefore, by interpolation we find that the precise internal rate of return AT is 19% + .64%, or 19.64%.

THE USE OF INCREMENTAL ANALYSIS

To determine the profitability of mutually exclusive projects of equal duration, it is advisable to use *incremental analysis*. With this procedure we analyze only the project that requires the least investment of capital, and compute the total net present value of the income by subtracting the present value of the investment (outflows) from that of the income (inflows). With each successive project that requires a greater investment, we need indicate only what incremental, or *additional*, amounts of outflows and inflows beyond those of the first project are involved. If, as may happen, the first project proves to be unsatisfactory, it is then not necessary to deal with the others.

Incremental analysis quickly distinguishes the more profitable projects from those less profitable. Three projects being considered by the LMN Corporation require investments of $10,000, $15,000 and $20,000 respectively. The results of incremental analysis are shown in Table 7-7. It is immediately evident from Table 7-7 that proportionately the most profitable project is Project A and that the incremental increase of inflows from Projects B and C will not produce nearly as high a degree of income.

TABLE 7-7.

| | *Project A* | *INCREMENTAL (ADDITIONAL) INCREASES* | |
		Project B	*Project C*
Total PV of outflows (investment)	$10,000	$ 5,000	$10,000
Total PV of inflows (income)	$25,000	$ 2,000	$ 5,000
Total net PV of income	$15,000	($ 3,000)	($ 5,000)

8

Capital Structure

THE MAIN TYPES OF CORPORATE CAPITAL

By definition, a firm's corporate capital structure is composed of those elements that go to make up its *long-term capital*. Hence, while the amount of short-term funds, such as those in accounts payable, accruals and reserves, may often be considerable, they are generally not considered part of the firm's capital structure.

The following three components constitute the basic capital structure of a corporation:

a. Long-term debt

b. Preferred stock

c. Common stock (or common stockholders' equity)

Each of these components has a great number of variations. Just as there are numerous forms of common and preferred stock, so debt may be in the form of mortgages, debentures, notes, convertible bonds, and so on.

NECESSARY CONSIDERATIONS WITH EACH FORM OF CAPITAL

A decision to employ corporate capital confronts the firm with important qualitative and quantitative considerations. In the main, these involve:

a. The payout each requires

b. Control by the existing management

c. The ultimate risk to the firm itself

Each different form of corporate capital selected raises somewhat different concerns.

Concerns with Long-term Debt

Payout: The company commits itself to fixed payments of interest and often the return of capital in the form of contributions to a sinking fund.

Control: Creditors may assume control of a company if it fails to meet its contractual obligations.

Risk: The prospect of defaulting on a debt is always a risk to the solvency of a company.

Concerns with Preferred Stock

Payout: The company commits itself to the payment of fixed dividends that have a prior claim on the company's earnings before common stock.

Control: Preferred stockholders may have the right to elect a certain number of members to the board of directors if the company fails to pay the preferred dividend.

Risk: The firm could be confronted by an arrearage of preferred stock dividends, preventing payment of cash dividends to common stockholders.

Concerns with Common Stock (or Common Stockholders' Equity)

Payout: After the claims of both debt and preferred stock are met, the common stockholders are entitled to all remaining earnings. By action of the board of directors, all or a portion of these may be retained by the firm or distributed in the form of cash dividends.

Control: The company is owned by the common stockholders, who have the legal right to determine all major policy decisions and to elect the board of directors. Thus, the owners of the majority of common stock wield ultimate control over the corporation and the number of shares outstanding bears directly upon corporate control. At the same time, stockholders have certain expectations about dividends, growth, and the like that, if not satisfied, may lead them to challenge the management's control.

Risk: An increase in the total common stock outstanding often dilutes the firm's earnings per share and hence the value of the common stock. Furthermore, as owners of the company, the common stockholders bear final responsibility for the firm.

DETERMINING THE COMPOSITION OF A FIRM'S CAPITAL STRUCTURE

A corporation determines what proportion of debt, preferred stock, and common stock should make up its capital structure. When there are no other external constraints, the firm makes its decision by weighing the relative advantages and disadvantages of using more or less of each type of capital. In making these decisions, concern with payout, control, and risk is fundamental, and careful consideration must be given to the questions they pose to the company. All of the following questions, in particular, should be examined carefully:

a.   The amount of the firm's annual burden of payments connected with interest, preferred stock dividends, contributions to sinking funds and other repayments of principal. [Question: Can the firm's income successfully carry the servicing of both debt and anticipated dividends?]

b.   The nature of cash flows in relation to capital needs. [Question: Will the company's cash flow enable it to meet its annual burden of debt and other demands? Or will additional short-term financing be required?]

c.   The relative cost of the different types of capital. Debt is usually the least expensive because there are tax-shielded savings on interest, whereas the use of common stock is the most expensive. [Question: To what extent does the firm's financial standing and credit enable it to employ less costly means of providing for its capital needs?]

d.   Maintaining control by management in the event that it undertakes capital financing by issuing common stock. [Question: Will a new stockholder majority select a different board of directors to replace current management?]

e.   Common stockholders' expectations with respect to dividends and capital gains, and the effects of the capital structure on both, particularly on the dilution of earnings. [Question: To what extent will stockholders express discontent with the firm's policies and thereby depress the price of the company's stock? This poses a real threat to the continuation of the existing management.]

f.   The company's desire for flexibility in future financing decisions. [Question: If more funds are needed later, will the current choice of a particular type of capital financing necessitate the use of some other, less desirable, form then?]

g.   The pattern of capital structure for the industry of which the firm is a part. [Question: To what extent must the firm's capital structure conform to the pattern followed by the industry as a whole?]

h. The degree of risk, especially with the use of bonds, when default could have the most serious consequences. [Question: Would a different form of capital financing, despite other disadvantages, pose less of a risk to the firm?]

i. The stability of the company's earnings, and therefore its ability to assume greater burdens for servicing debt. [Question: Are the firm's anticipated earnings reasonably assured in the years ahead, or are they subject to considerable fluctuation that could create great risk in meeting fiscal obligations?]

j. The desire for more financial leverage, which encourages greater use of debt. [Question: In view of the added risk, will the firm's common stockholders really enjoy greater earnings by increasing the amount of debt?]

k. Market conditions that could dictate the use of one form of capital rather than another. [Question: Are current interest rates prohibitively high? Or what is the general receptivity of the public to common or preferred stock offerings?]

l. Subjective factors that might contribute to the decision, such as management's personal preference for short-term rather than long-term financing. [Question: Are the stature and financial capacity of the firm such that the general public will accept whatever form of capital financing management chooses?]

THE FINANCIAL BREAK-EVEN POINT

A basic factor in the decision-making about which form of capital to employ is the sum the firm is trying to raise. Whatever type of capital it chooses, the firm must know two things: (a) The amount of bonds or stock that must be issued to raise this capital, and (b) the additional burden the company must then carry. The answer to both questions may be found by using the *financial break-even point,* also called the *indifference point.* Essentially, the financial break-even point indicates at what point the use of different types of capital will be of equal cost.

The following equation expresses the amount of earnings before interest and taxes (EBIT) needed to cover the burden of all three major types of long-term capital financing without diluting the earnings of the common stockholders. Once this amount is determined, it is comparatively easy to calculate the total amount the firm must raise if it is to meet its financial needs within the burden it is assuming.

With Bonds and Preferred Stock

$$\frac{[(1 - t) \times (EBIT - i)] - P}{n}$$

With Common Stock

$$\frac{[(1 - t) \times (EBIT - i)] - P}{n}$$

In which:

$EBIT$ = earnings before interest and taxes

i = the total amount of interest to be paid, both current and anticipated

t = tax rate

P = preferred dividends, both current and anticipated

n = the number of common shares, both current and anticipated

Assume that at the start of 1977 the LMN Corporation contemplates raising $100 million to finance a project. Below are calculations of the LMN Corporation's break-even point for bonds, preferred stock, and common stock. (For simplicity, we ignore all broker, legal, and other fees customarily associated with capital financing.) Note that raising the needed $100 million by selling bonds at 6% will produce an additional annual expense of $6 million in interest paid to the bond-holders. Preferred stock paying $5 will cost the firm $5 million more annually. And use of common stock presently selling at $70 a share will necessitate issuing approximately 1,430,000 additional shares.

(millions of dollars)

With Bonds | With Common Stock

$$\frac{[(1-t) \times (EBIT - i)] - P}{n} = \frac{[(1-t) \times (EBIT - i)] - P}{n}$$

$$\frac{[(1-.48) \times (EBIT - \$2.25 + \$6)] - \$.1}{4 \text{ million shares}} = \frac{[(1-.48) \times (EBIT - \$2.25)] - \$.1}{5.43 \text{ million shares}}$$

$$\frac{[(.52) \times (EBIT - \$8.25)] - \$.1}{4 \text{ million shares}} = \frac{[(.52) \times (EBIT - \$2.25)] - \$.1}{5.43 \text{ million shares}}$$

$$\frac{.52\,EBIT - \$4.39}{4 \text{ million shares}} = \frac{.52\,EBIT - \$1.27}{5.43 \text{ million shares}}$$

$$.13\,EBIT - \$1.10 = .10\,EBIT - \$.23$$

$$EBIT = \$29$$

With Preferred Stock | With Common Stock

$$\frac{[(1-t) \times (EBIT - i)] - P}{n} = \frac{[(1-t) \times (EBIT - i)] - P}{n}$$

$$\frac{[(1-.48) \times (EBIT - \$2.25)] - (\$.1 + \$5)}{4 \text{ million shares}} = \frac{[(1-.48) \times (EBIT - \$2.25)] - \$.1}{5.43 \text{ million shares}}$$

$$\frac{.52\,EBIT - \$6.27}{4 \text{ million shares}} = \frac{.52\,EBIT - \$1.27}{5.43 \text{ million shares}}$$

$$.13\,EBIT - \$1.57 = .10\,EBIT - \$.23$$

$$EBIT = \$44.7$$

Our calculations show that in relation to floating more common stock, the financial break-even point associated with the issuance of new bonds is at an earnings level BIT of $29 million. The earnings level BIT is $44.7 million for new preferred stock. On the basis of this information, if it is fiscally possible, the LMN Corporation will raise its $100 million by issuing bonds.

9

The Cost of Capital

WHAT IS THE REAL COST OF CORPORATE CAPITAL?

Corporate capital structure, as we have observed, is composed of three major elements: debt, preferred stock, and common stock (common stockholders' equity). It is plain, therefore, that the firm's cost for the use of capital is the sum of the expense of each of these three elements.

While it is clear that debt has its cost in the form of interest, and preferred stock in terms of regular dividends, common stock is also not without its cost. The most obvious cost is the dividends paid to common stockholders. But there are also *opportunity costs* involved in the use of such equity funds as paid-in capital and accumulated retained earnings, which belong to the stockholders as owners of the corporation. What percentage of income, for instance, are the stockholders and the management forgoing by not investing these funds in ventures outside the company? And is the firm realizing an adequate percentage of return from the application of such funds to its various enterprises? Surely, as part of the total cost of corporate capital, all this must be considered in connection with the use of common stockholders' equity.

DETERMINING AN APPROPRIATE DISCOUNT RATE

By calculating the firm's cost of capital, we are enabled to decide what interest rate (or *discount rate*) we are justified in using. Interest rates, of course, are integral to the cost of debt and preferred stock. But equity funds belonging to the common stockholder are no less subject to discount rates. And since the two principal methods of capital budgeting—net present value and the internal rate of return—employ a predetermined discount rate, the cost of capital cannot be computed without some basic agreement as to what that discount rate is.

70

What is an acceptable discount rate? The following are often used as guidelines:

a.   The current interest rate the firm must pay in order to borrow money.

b.   The percent of profit normally achieved by the firm.

c.   The *hurdle rate*, or the predetermined rate of return that the firm decides it must exceed if it is to undertake a project.

d.   The *opportunity cost* of funds, or how much the firm could earn by investing its money elsewhere, as expressed by a percentage.

e.   The weighted average cost AT of the firm's capital.

In general, the firm's weighted average cost of capital AT is most widely accepted as the appropriate discount rate of a firm.

THE WEIGHTED AVERAGE AFTER-TAX COST OF CAPITAL

The weighted average cost of capital AT is composed of the sum of:

a.   The weighted cost of debt capital AT;

b.   The weighted cost of preferred stock; and

c.   The weighted cost of common stockholders' equity.

These component costs may be calculated on the basis of either their book value or their market value, although the market value reflects current, and consequently more realistic, values. The weighted average cost of the LMN Corporation's capital, based on 1976 figures, can similarly be computed in either of two ways, depending on whether we use book value (Table 9-1) or market value (Table 9-2).

TABLE 9-1.
(thousands of dollars)

Type of Capital	Details	Total Amount	Proportion of Total Amount	Cost AT $(t = .48)$	Weighted Cost
Long-term debt	Bonds of $37,500 at 6%	$ 37,500	29.9%	$(1 - .48)$ .031 $[6\% \times .52]$	29.9% $\times$ .031 $=$ .009

TABLE 9-1. (continued)
(thousands of dollars)

Type of Capital	Details	Total Amount	Proportion of Total Amount	Cost AT (t = .48)	Weighted Cost
Preferred stock	20,000 shares at $100 par paying $5 dividend	$ 2,000	1.6%	.050	1.6% × .050 = .008
Common stock- holder's equity:					
Common shares	4 million shares at $1.25 par $5,000				
Capital surplus	$12,050	$ 85,800	68.5%	.060*	68.5% × .060 = .041
Accum- ulated retained income	$68,750				
Net total		$125,300	100.0%		.058 or 5.8%

*The cost of common stockholders' equity remains the same whether book value or market value is used because the percentage is based upon the earnings per share (EPS) divided by the market price per share (PPS).

Therefore the 6% cost of common stockholders' equity for the LMN Corporation in 1976 was arrived at as follows:

$$\text{Earnings per share (EPS)} = \frac{\$16.85 \text{ million (NAT)}}{4 \text{ million (shares outstanding)}} = \$4.21$$

The cost of capital for its common stockholders' equity *(K)* is thus:

$$K = \frac{\$4.21 \text{ (EPS)}}{\$70 \text{ (PPS)}} = .060, \text{ or } 6\%$$

TABLE 9-2.
(thousands of dollars)

Type of Capital	Details	Total Amount	Proportion of Total Amount	Cost AT (t = .48)	Weighted Cost
Long-term debt	Bonds of $37,500 at 6%	$ 38,250*	12.0%	(1 − .48) .031 [6% × .52]	.004
Preferred stock	20,000 shares at $100 par paying $5 dividend	$ 2,000	0.6%	.05	.003
Common shares	4 million shares at $70 PPS	$280,000	87.4%	.06	.052
Net total		$320,250	100.0%		.059 or 5.9%

*The market value of the company's bonds has appreciated from a book value of $37.5 million to $38.25 million.

ESTABLISHING THE COST OF CAPITAL FOR COMMON STOCKHOLDERS' EQUITY

There are five principal ways to determine the cost of capital for common stockholders' equity. The results will be subject to considerable variation, depending upon which method is used.

a. One way of determining the cost of capital for common stockholder's equity is to divide earnings per share (EPS) by the market price per share (PPS).

$$K = \frac{\text{Earnings Per Share (EPS)}}{\text{Price Per Share (PPS)}} = \frac{\$4.21}{\$70} = .060, \text{ or } 6\%$$

b. A second method involves dividing the net earnings AT, minus the preferred dividends, by the total stockholders' equity (net worth), or in brief.

$$K = \frac{\text{Net Earnings AT} - \text{Preferred Dividends}}{\text{Total Stockholders' Equity (Net Worth)}}$$

In the case of the LMN Corporation for 1976 the cost of capital for common stockholders' equity, calculated this way, is:

$$\frac{\$16,850,000 - \$100,000}{\$87,800,000} = \frac{\$16,750,000}{\$87,800,000} = .191, \text{ or } 19.1\%$$

c. Dividing the common stock dividend per share by the market price per share (PPS) and adding an estimated growth factor *(g)*, which is considered the rate of the growth of the firm's dividends translated into the stockmarket price, is another approach.

$$K = \frac{\text{Common Stock Dividend Per Share}}{\text{Market Price Per Share (PPS)}} + \text{growth } (g)$$

In the case of the LMN Corporation for 1976 this would be:

$$\frac{\$.45 \text{ (common stock dividend per share)}}{\$70 \text{ (PPS)}} + g \text{ (growth)}$$

The growth factor *(g)* for 1975–1976 will be the rate of change in earnings per share in 1976 compared with earnings per share in 1975, assumed here to be $3.50. Therefore, *g* is:

$$\frac{\$4.21 \text{ (EPS in 1976)}}{\$3.50 \text{ (EPS in 1975)}} = .202 \ (g)$$

Therefore, in 1976 the LMN Corporation's total cost of equity capital *(K)* is:

$$\frac{\$.45 \text{ (common stock dividend per share)}}{\$70 \text{ (market price per share)}} + .202 \ (g)$$

$$= .006 + .202 = .208, \text{ or } 20.8\%$$

d. Another means of determining the cost of capital for common stockholders' equity is by calculating the average productivity of the firm's assets before interest but after taxes. To do this, we divide the firm's average income BI but AT by its average total assets, or

$$K = \frac{\text{Average Income BI but AT}}{\text{Average Total Assets}}$$

In the case of the LMN Corporation in 1976, the cost of equity capital would be:

$$\frac{\frac{1}{2} \ (\$19,100 \ [1976] + \$16,565 \ [1975])}{\frac{1}{2} \ (\$187,300 \ [1976] + \$172,300 \ [1975])} = \frac{\$17,833}{\$179,800}$$

$$= .099, \text{ or } 9.9\%$$

e. The most widely accepted method of determining the cost of common stock-holders' equity is to compute the weighted average cost of its two chief components; namely: (1) the weighted cost of issuing new common stock, plus (2) the weighted cost of common equity funds internally-generated through both retained income and depreciation. The following equations are used to determine the costs of the various components.

(1) The weighted cost of issuing new common stock is:

$$\frac{R}{(1 - F)} \times (C + S)$$

In which:

R = the firm's required rate of return
F = the expense of floating new common shares
C = the book value of the firm's common stock
S = book value of the firm's "surplus" or paid-in capital

(2) The weighted cost of internally-generated common equity funds is:

$$R \times (1 - t_{cg}) \times (RI + D)*$$

In which:

R = the firm's required rate of return
t_{cg} = personal tax-rate for capital gains
RI = the firm's accumulated retained income
D = the firm's depreciation for the year

In each case, after the results are obtained they are multiplied by percentages representing the proportionate amounts of both components. The sum of the two is thus considered to be the firm's weighted average cost of capital for common stockholders' equity *(K)*. The weighted average cost of capital based on book value for common stockholders' equity in the LMN Corporation in 1976 is computed as shown in Table 9-3.

*Some financial analysts suggest that, as with the first component above—the weighted cost of issuing new common stock—and as a necessary part of the total expense, the weighted cost of internally-generated common equity funds should also be divided by $(1 - F)$, in which F is the cost of floating new common shares.

TABLE 9-3.

(thousands of dollars)

[For explanation of symbols see text]

Components of Equity Capital	Total Amount: LMN Corporation 1976	Proportion of Total Amount	Determination of Cost Assumptions: $R = 7\%,\ F = 20\%,$ $t_{cg} = 25\%$	Weighted Cost
New com- mon stock	$ 5,000 *(C)* 12,050 *(S)* $17,050	14.5%	$\dfrac{R}{(1-F)} = \dfrac{7\%}{1-20\%}$ $= \dfrac{.07}{.80} = .0875$	.145 × .0875 = .013
Funds inter- nally- generated	$ 68,750 *(RI)* 31,500 *(D)* $100,250	85.5%	$R \times (1 - t_{cg}) =$ $7\% \times (1 - 25\%)$ $= .0525$ [If also div- ided by $(1 - F)$ or .80, the result would be .0656. For weighted costs incorpor- ating this figure see the bracketed figures in the final column.]	.855 × .0525 = .045 [.056]
Net total	$117,300	100.0%		.058 or 5.8% [6.9%]

Table 9-3 shows that in 1976 the LMN Corporation's weighted average cost of capital for common stockholders' equity *(K)* is 5.8%. This represents the sum of the weighted average cost of its (1) common stock and "surplus" or paid-in capital, plus (2) its accumulated retained income and the value of the year's depreciation. Note how closely this figure corresponds to the one of 6% arrived at by dividing earnings per share (EPS) by market price per share (PPS) in the footnote on page 72.

10

Considerations with Mergers

SOME PRELIMINARY QUESTIONS OF IMPORTANCE

When we first introduced the LMN Corporation, the firm was facing a decision on whether it should introduce a new line of merchandise. It also had the associated option of purchasing the smaller RS Company, which already manufactures the product under consideration. Opportunities for merger arise frequently in corporate life, and, as with most other phases of financial analysis, determining the desirability of such a move demands careful preliminary evaluation of a considerable number of qualitative and quantitative questions. Among the most important of these questions are the following:

a. What is the acquiring firm seeking? Multiple answers are possible. Sometimes a merger may represent a desire for growth. Or the firm may be interested in purchasing another company for its technological skills, complementary products and outlets, managerial personnel, or even for a temporary tax loss.

b. What is the company-to-be-acquired seeking? Sometimes merger with a larger firm seems the best solution to the need for financing or better management. Or, for estate-tax purposes, merger could be the simplest way of establishing the value of a family-controlled business. And if the owners face the prospect of having to discontinue operating, they will stand to benefit far more from selling the company intact than they would from liquidating it.

c. Is the merger legal? Does it pose any possible violation of the anti-trust laws?

d. How much will the merger improve the financial situation of the company-to-be-acquired?

e. How will the merger affect the dividends paid to the common stockholders of both companies?

f. What effect will the merger have on the cash flow of the acquiring company?

g. What price will the acquiring firm have to pay for the company-to-be-acquired?

h. Does the company-to-be-acquired possess any assets that the acquiring company might sell in order to reduce the purchase price or to minimize a potential financial drain created by the merger?

i. How will the acquiring company finance the merger, and what effect will the method it chooses have on its capital structure?

Answers to some of these questions, such as the legality of the merger and the basic objectives of the two companies, are essentially qualitative in nature. Others are quantitative and require detailed financial analysis. One quantitative question is, What is the company-to-be-acquired really worth?

FIVE MEANS OF DETERMINING THE VALUE OF A COMPANY

Different financial experts suggest varying ways of determining the value of a company, and not surprisingly, each method produces a somewhat different result. For the purpose of illustration, we shall present five of the most frequently recommended techniques and then apply each to the situation

TABLE 10-1.

Current assets	$6 million
Current liabilities	$4.5 million
Other (long-term) assets	$12 million
Long-term liabilities	$4 million
Preferred stock	none
Common stock	.5 million shares
Book value of common stockholders' equity	$9.5 million
Market value per common share	$20
Total market value of common shares	$10 million
Earnings AT per share	$2.00
Dividends per share	$.50
Total current earnings AT	$1 million
Average earnings AT over past 3 years	$.9 million
Average annual increase in earnings	$.1 million

involving the possible merger of the LMN Corporation with the RS Company. We shall need to keep in mind the basic information about the RS Company presented in Table 10-1.

The Book Value of a Company's Net Worth

The book value of the net worth of the company-to-be-acquired sometimes determines its purchase price. Net worth, we recall, is the total value of the preferred and common stockholders' equity as it appears in the financial position statement. Since the RS Company has no preferred stock, its net worth is the book value of the common stockholders' equity, in this instance $9.5 million. Often—especially when prices have appreciated—if only book value is being considered, the worth of a company-to-be-acquired will be understated.

The Market Value of a Company's Net Worth

The market value of the net worth of the company-to-be-acquired may also be used to establish a purchase price. This is computed by adding the price of the company's preferred shares times their number to the price of its common shares times their number outstanding. Thus, the market value of the company's net worth is:

(Price per Preferred Share × Number of Preferred Shares Outstanding) + (Price per Common Share × Number of Common Shares Outstanding)

The market value of the RS Company's net worth is $10 million. This amount was arrived at by calculating: (0 [preferred shares outstanding] × 0 [price per preferred share]) + $20 [market value per common share]) × .5 million (common shares outstanding) = $10 million.

The Liquidation Value of a Company

The minimum price of a company-to-be-acquired is often assumed to be its liquidation value. To find the liquidation value, we first compute (a) the worth of the company's working capital per share by dividing the total working capital (CA − CL) by the number of common shares outstanding. Next we calculate (b) the estimated worth of the firm's other long-term assets less its long-term liabilities and the value of its outstanding preferred stock. We divide the result by the number of common shares outstanding. The sum of (a) and (b) is the liquidation value of the company.

$$V = \frac{(CA - CL)}{n} + \frac{Lt\,A - (Lt\,L + P)}{n}$$

In which:

$$V = \text{value of the firm}$$
$$Lt\,A = \text{long-term assets}$$
$$Lt\,B = \text{long-term liabilities}$$
$$P = \text{preferred stock outstanding}$$
$$CA - CL = \text{working capital}$$
$$n = \text{number of common shares}$$

By applying this formula to the RS Company, assuming that its long-term assets are saleable at 37.5% of their stated value, we find that the company's liquidation value is $2 million.

$$V = \frac{\$6\text{ million} - \$4.5\text{ million}}{.5\text{ million}} + \frac{(.375 \times \$12\text{ million}) - (\$4\text{ million} + 0)}{.5\text{ million}}$$

$$= \frac{\$1.5\text{ million}}{.5\text{ million}} + \frac{\$4.5\text{ million} - \$4\text{ million}}{.5\text{ million}}$$

$$= \frac{\$2\text{ million}}{.5\text{ million}}, \text{ or } \$4 \text{ per share}$$

A firm's liquidation value will, obviously, be considerably lower than its worth as a going concern. The *replacement value*, or the worth of the company's assets at current prices, is sometimes used to produce a higher, more reasonable figure.

The Capitalization Value of Average Historical Earnings

A fourth method of determining the worth of a company-to-be-acquired is to capitalize its average historical earnings at the discount rate of the acquiring company's cost of capital. To this, however, allowance must also be made for probable changes in future earnings as well as any possible risk *(margin of safety)* factor.* In simplified form, this method is expressed as:

$$V = \frac{E \pm g}{i + R}$$

In which:

$$V = \text{value of the firm}$$
$$E = \text{the company-to-be-acquired's average historical earnings}$$

*Generally, a risk factor of several percent is added to the discount rate to compensate for the estimated additional risk to an investor in the company's bonds as compared to an investor in high-rated government securities. When assumptions about future income, expenses, residual values and the like create even greater uncertainty, a still larger percentage is added.

g = percent of probable change in earnings, or "growth rate"

i = cost of capital or "discount rate" of the acquiring firm

R = possible risk, or "margin of safety," factor, here assumed to be 2%

By capitalizing the value of the average historical earnings of the RS Company, we establish a purchase price of $12.5 million:

$$V = \frac{\$.9 \text{ million} + \$.1 \text{ million}}{6\% + 2\%}$$

$$= \frac{\$1.0 \text{ million}}{.08}$$

$$= \$12.5 \text{ million}$$

The Present Value of Average Future Worth

Finally, we can use the present value of a company-to-be-acquired's average future worth over a limited number of years as its purchase price. This value is determined by adding together the present values of its average earnings projected over the anticipated time-period, the estimated average annual change in the company's income, and the residual value of the company, then subtracting the worth of the firm's preferred stock from that sum. The rate used for calculating present values over the anticipated time-period is that of the acquiring company's cost of capital (or discount rate).

$$V = [(PV \text{ of } E_p) \pm (PV \text{ of } g) + (PV \text{ of } V_r)] - P$$

In which:

V = value of the firm

E_p = average earnings of the company-to-be-acquired projected over the time period

g = amount of probable change in earnings, or "growth rate"

V_r = residual value of the firm at end of the time period

i = cost of capital or "discount rate" of the acquiring company

P = total value of all preferred stock outstanding

Let us postpone consideration of the present value of V_r (residual value of the RS Company) for the moment, and begin calculating the present value of the average future earnings of the RS Company. Because of some predetermined considerations, we have decided to project the company's earnings horizon for eight years. We will use the LMN Corporation's discount rate of 6%.

We temporarily omit $(PV \text{ of } V_r)$ and P from the equation given previously, and proceed to supply the data for

$$[(PV \text{ of } E_p) \pm (PV \text{ of } g)]$$

PV of E_p (projected average earnings) $= PV$ of $1 million
   $= $1 million $\times$ 6.21 (the present value of an annuity of $1, where $n = 8$
      and $i = 6\%$)
   $= $6.21 million

PV of g (average annual change) $= PV$ of $100,000
   $= $100,000 $\times$ 6.21 (the present value of an annuity of $1, where $n = 8$
      and $i = 6\%$)
   $= $.621 million in growth

So $[(PV$ of $E_p) \pm (PV$ of $g)] = $6.21 million $+ $.621 million, or $6.831 million.

Now we must return to the matter of the present value of V_r (residual value). Clearly, it will not be easy to determine what worth the RS Company will still possess for the LMN Corporation eight years from now. Many options are possible. We could reach some conclusion after carefully considering the present value of each of the RS Company's long-term assets. Or we could assume that the production of the RS Company would still provide a certain amount of income and calculate the present value of that estimate. Or, by taking into account other variables such as inflation, replacement values, and so forth, we could simply assign an arbitrary sum that we consider a reasonable residual value for the firm after eight years. These are only some of the possibilities.

Clearly, a projection presents considerable risk. Therefore, we will add on a special R (risk factor) of 4% to the 6% discount rate that we have been using. We thus have a new, 10% discount rate to use when dealing with the present value of V_r (residual value).

Let us operate on the assumption that the residual value of the RS Company will be the present value of both (1) the net of its earnings over the previous eight year period ($6.831 million) and (2) the worth of certain long-term assets totaling $4,500 million at that point. Thus,

$(PV$ of $V_r)$ (residual value) $= PV$ of $6,831 million (earnings over the previous
      8 years) $+ PV$ of $4,500 million (estimated re-
      sidual worth of long-term assets)
   $= PV$ of $11.331 million
   $= .467$ (the present value of $1 where $n = 8$ and i
      $+R = 10$) $\times$ $11.331 million
   $= $5.292 million

After returning to our original equation, which was

V (Value of the firm) $= [(PV$ of $E_p) \pm (PV$ of $g) + (PV$ of $V_r)] - P$,

we are able to complete our calculations as follows:

V (Value of the firm) $= $6.831 million $[(PV$ of $E_p) \pm (PV$ of $g)] + $5.292
      million $[(PV$ of $V_r)] - 0(P)$

$$= \$12.123 \text{ million} - 0$$
$$= \$12.123 \text{ million}$$

The Conclusion: A Likely Compromise

It is clear that, in a merger, the value assigned to the company-to-be-acquired may vary widely, depending upon the method used to determine it. In virtually all cases, the lowest figure is based on the firm's liquidation value. Often, too, book value will fail to represent a current, and therefore realistic, estimate of the firm's worth. But even if market value is used, the financial conditions prevailing during a particular period may distort the price.

There are, moreover, special difficulties with each of the other methods. Utilizing either the capitalization of the firm's average historical earnings or the present value of its future earnings involves using a number of variables that are uncertain. The discount rate, for example, which is used in determining the anticipated annual rate of change in income, the percent of possible risk, and the optimal time-period, is such an uncertain variable. Consequently, results achieved by using these factors are also open to question.

In the final analysis, the value of a firm is usually established through a compromise of the results obtained from the use of several methods. Naturally, the seller will employ those methods whose results will encourage a higher price for the company, while the purchaser will adopt those methods that support a lower one. So, in the case of the LMN Corporation's contemplated acquisition of the RS Company, the proposed prices range from a low of $2 million, based on liquidation value, to a high of $12.5 million, obtained by using the capitalization value of average historical earnings. It is likely that through negotiations a compromise will be reached somewhere within the middle to upper range of estimates, which extend from the $9.5 million of book value or the $10 million market value to the $12.123 million representing the present value of average future worth or the $12.5 million based on the capitalization of average historical earnings.

COMPUTING DATA OF SIGNIFICANCE AS THE RESULT OF A MERGER

Whatever price is finally agreed upon, we now have the answers to most of the remaining quantitative questions. For example, we are in a position to know the merger's effect upon the earnings and dividends of the surviving company, and what, consequently, the new value of the common shares will be. So, assuming that the LMN Corporation is finally prepared to merge with the RS Company, let us suppose that the agreed formula for acquiring the RS Company is that the LMN Corporation will pay the stockholders one share of LMN common stock for every three shares of RS stock. We can thus arrive at the following facts: The value of the RS Company is $11.67 million because each LMN share is worth $70 and ⅓ of $70, the new value of an RS Share, is $23.33. This price per share times the .5 million RS shares outstanding produces a total amount of $11.67 million. On the basis of this information, we can now determine the merged corporation's new number of common shares outstanding and its total current earnings AT. In Table 10-2, a summary of data for the RS and LMN firms, this information is given in the line headed "Totals for the merged firm."

TABLE 10-2.

Company	Price Per Share	Earnings Per Share AT	Dividends Per Share	Number of Shares	New Number of Shares	Total Current Earnings AT
LMN Corporation (the acquiring company)	$70	$4.21	$.45	4 million	4 million	$16.85 million
RS Company (the company to-be-acquired)	$20	$2.00	$.50	5 million	.167 million	$1.0 million
Totals for the merged firm					4.167 million	$17.85 million

The information given in Table 10-2 also reveals that:

The original price-earnings ratio of the LMN Corporation was $70/$4.21, or 16.6.

The original PE ratio of the RS Company was $20/$2.00, or 10.

The new earnings per share will be $17.85 million/4.167 million shares = $4.28.

The value of a new share of the merged LMN Corporation stock will be $71.05. This is computed by multiplying 16.6 (the firm's original PE ratio) by $4.28 (the new EPS for the merged corporation).

Since it will require three shares of RS Company stock to obtain one share of LMN Corporation common, the value of each new share of stock to the shareholder of the RS Company will now be ⅓ of $71.05 (the new share's value), or $23.68.

The LMN Corporation's price-earnings ratio will continue to be 16.6. This PE is obtained by dividing $71.05 (the new PPS) by $4.28 (the new EPS).

At a price per share of $23.68, the value of the RS Company's stock is slightly more than 5.5 times the merged corporation's new per-share earnings of $4.28.

The original dividend-to-earnings ratio of the LMN Corporation was 10.68%. This is obtained by dividing $1.8 million, the total amount of the firm's common dividend, by $16.85 million, its net earnings AT. (Virtually the same result is obtained by dividing $.45, the dividend per share, by $4.21, the earnings-per-share.)

By applying the new dividends-to-earnings ratio of 10.68% to the EPS AT of the merged company (10.68% × $4.28), we find that the new dividend to LMN Corporation stockholders has increased from $.45 to $.46.

Note, then, the effects of the merger upon the common stockholders of both companies as shown in Table 10-3.

TABLE 10-3.

	LMN Corporation	RS Company
Price per share	Increases from $70 to $71.05	Increases from $20 to $23.68
Earnings per share	Increases from $4.21 to $4.28	Decreases from 3 times $2.00 ($6.00) to $4.28
Price-earnings ratio	Remains constant at 16.6	Decreases from 10 to slightly more than 5.5
Dividend per share	Increases from $.45 to $.46	Decreases from 3 times $.50 ($1.50) to $.46

Further Readings

CHAPTER 1. THE BASIC FINANCIAL DOCUMENTS

Bogen, Jules I., ed. 1968. *Financial Handbook*. New York: The Ronald Press Company.

This encyclopedic book, which covers special topics in the field of finance, is a classic reference work. It is definitive, taxonomic, and highly detailed, yet it is written for all members of the financial community. *Financial Handbook* is written by experts in subjects ranging from financial statement analysis to merger and consolidation and contains theoretical and practical wisdom in a highly workable reference format.

Helfert, Eric A. 1972. *Techniques of Financial Analysis*. Homewood, Ill.: Richard D. Irwin, Inc.

Techniques of Financial Analysis provides a concise reference collection of important tools and techniques of financial analysis and is burdened with little theoretical and institutional background. This work emphasizes the topics of funds flow analysis, pro forma financial statements and their use, analysis of funds sources, and basic capital investment decisions.

Wright, Leonard. 1974. *Financial Management: Analytical Techniques*. Columbus, Ohio: GRID, Inc.

In this book, which is keyed to the variety of financial problems of business operations, Wright provides detailed techniques for use by business managers and students of finance at several levels of skills. Topics covered range from daily operating financial problems to episodic activities in capital source and capital investment decision-making.

CHAPTER 2. THE METHOD OF DEALING WITH A CASE — AN OVERVIEW

Weston, J. Fred. 1966. *The Scope and Methodology of Finance*. Englewood Cliffs, N.J.: Prentice-Hall, Inc.

The *Scope and Methodology of Finance* is a pioneer work in that it defines the range of analytical skills that are needed for one to practice finance in modern enterprise.

While highly theoretical, the book is helpful to both the analyst and the practitioner of financial management.

CHAPTER 3. COMMON-SIZE ANALYSIS AND OTHER MEASURES OF A FIRM'S FINANCIAL STATE

Brigham, Eugene F. and Weston, J. Fred. 1974. *Managerial Finance*. Englewood Cliffs, N.J.: Prentice-Hall, Inc.

Managerial Finance is an advanced level text. A major feature of this authoritative work is the emphasis given to techniques of analyzing risk. After providing a strong framework based on the classical doctrines in finance, the authors present materials on important and controversial issues that currently face today's financial managers.

Hunt, Pearson, Williams, Charles M., and Donaldson, Gordon. 1971. *Basic Business Finance: Text and Cases*. Homewood, Ill.: Richard D. Irwin, Inc.

The main asset of this book is that it provides both textual materials covering major topics in financial management and case examples giving problems for practical solution. The book's focus on the decision-making financial officer in a business firm provides the context for its presentation of theory and lends relevance to its discussions of financial decisions. The economical and effective use of funds is the underlying concern of the authors.

CHAPTER 4. THE TIME-VALUE OF MONEY

Black, Homer A. 1973. *Accounting in Business Decisions: Theory, Method and Use*. Englewood Cliffs, N.J.: Prentice-Hall, Inc.

Accounting in Business Decisions shows how accounting provides the frame of reference, finite figures, and measurement data used in business decision-making. Theory and application are skillfully meshed to emphasize the clear need for accurate and appropriate accounting information in supporting business managers in making risk-oriented decisions.

CHAPTER 5. INTEREST RATES, TRADE DISCOUNTS, AND BOND VALUES

Ayres, Frank Jr. 1967. *Theory and Problems of Mathematics of Finance* (Schaum's Outline Series). New York: McGraw-Hill Book Company.

This book is a precise, complete work on the mathematics needed for financial administration. Basic business commercial mathematics, financial instruments mathematics, present-value techniques, and the mathematics of annuities are covered. The book also contains particularly valuable tables.

Cohen, Jerome B., Zinbarg, Edward D., and Zeikel, Arthur. 1973. *Investment Analysis and Portfolio Management*. Homewood, Ill.: Richard D. Irwin, Inc.

Investment Analysis and Portfolio Management is a wide-ranging and sophisticated analysis of investment theories and their applicability to real world investment and portfolio management practices. Controversial areas of accounting measurements of investment data, technical analysis of securities markets, institutional investment trends, and the quantitative revolution in investment analysis are carefully examined in extreme detail. This is a complete and brave book of considerable stature and utility.

CHAPTER 6. TAXES, DEPRECIATION, AND BUY OR LEASE DECISIONS

Bierman, Harold Jr. and Smidt, Seymour. 1975. *The Capital Budgeting Decision*. New York: MacMillan, Inc.

For many years, *The Capital Budgeting Decision* has been a standard work on the construction of analytical techniques and their application to capital investment decisions. In this latest edition, the authors press into new ground of cost of capital theory and application in the risk-oriented capital decisions facing modern business managers. Its skillful combining of theory, practice, and examples makes this work a reference for advanced analysis.

CHAPTER 7. CAPITAL BUDGETING

Merrett, A. J. and Sykes, Allen. 1974. *The Finance and Analysis of Capital Projects*. Essex, England: Longman Group, Ltd.

This book provides a complete and detailed exposition of the best practice-proven techniques of appraising long-term capital investments. Discussion of the relevant theories of capital budgeting are buttressed by sophisticated examples of successful use of these techniques. The problems of financing long-term capital investments, a feature neglected in most advanced works, are also given considerable attention in this study.

Appendixes: Present Value Tables

TABLE 1:   The Amount of $1 (The Value [or Amount] to Which $1 Adds Up in the Future If It Is Invested Today at Compound Interest):
$V = S \times n]i$

n	¾%	1%	1¼%	1½%	1¾%	2%	n
1	1.008	1.010	1.013	1.015	1.018	1.020	1
2	1.015	1.020	1.025	1.030	1.035	1.040	2
3	1.023	1.030	1.038	1.046	1.053	1.061	3
4	1.030	1.041	1.051	1.061	1.072	1.082	4
5	1.038	1.051	1.064	1.077	1.091	1.104	5
6	1.046	1.062	1.077	1.093	1.110	1.126	6
7	1.054	1.072	1.091	1.110	1.129	1.149	7
8	1.062	1.083	1.105	1.127	1.149	1.172	8
9	1.070	1.094	1.118	1.143	1.169	1.195	9
10	1.078	1.105	1.132	1.161	1.190	1.219	10
11	1.086	1.116	1.146	1.178	1.210	1.243	11
12	1.094	1.127	1.161	1.196	1.231	1.268	12
13	1.102	1.138	1.175	1.213	1.253	1.294	13
14	1.110	1.150	1.190	1.232	1.275	1.320	14
15	1.119	1.161	1.205	1.250	1.297	1.346	15
16	1.127	1.173	1.220	1.269	1.320	1.373	16
17	1.136	1.184	1.235	1.288	1.343	1.400	17
18	1.144	1.196	1.251	1.307	1.367	1.428	18
19	1.153	1.208	1.266	1.327	1.391	1.457	19
20	1.161	1.220	1.282	1.347	1.415	1.486	20
21	1.170	1.232	1.298	1.367	1.440	1.516	21
22	1.179	1.245	1.314	1.388	1.465	1.546	22
23	1.188	1.257	1.331	1.409	1.490	1.577	23
24	1.196	1.270	1.347	1.430	1.516	1.608	24
25	1.205	1.282	1.364	1.451	1.543	1.641	25
26	1.214	1.295	1.381	1.473	1.570	1.673	26
27	1.224	1.308	1.399	1.495	1.598	1.707	27
28	1.233	1.321	1.416	1.517	1.625	1.741	28
29	1.242	1.334	1.434	1.540	1.654	1.776	29
30	1.251	1.348	1.452	1.563	1.683	1.811	30
31	1.261	1.361	1.470	1.587	1.712	1.848	31
32	1.270	1.375	1.488	1.610	1.742	1.885	32
33	1.280	1.389	1.507	1.635	1.773	1.922	33
34	1.289	1.403	1.526	1.659	1.804	1.961	34
35	1.300	1.417	1.545	1.684	1.835	2.000	35
36	1.309	1.431	1.564	1.709	1.867	2.040	36
37	1.319	1.445	1.584	1.735	1.900	2.081	37
38	1.328	1.460	1.603	1.761	1.933	2.122	38
39	1.338	1.474	1.623	1.787	1.967	2.165	39
40	1.348	1.489	1.644	1.814	2.002	2.208	40
41	1.359	1.504	1.664	1.841	2.037	2.252	41
42	1.369	1.519	1.685	1.869	2.072	2.297	42
43	1.379	1.534	1.706	1.897	2.109	2.343	43
44	1.389	1.550	1.727	1.925	2.145	2.390	44
45	1.400	1.565	1.749	1.954	2.183	2.438	45
46	1.410	1.581	1.771	1.984	2.221	2.487	46
47	1.421	1.596	1.793	2.013	2.260	2.536	47
48	1.431	1.612	1.815	2.044	2.300	2.587	48
49	1.442	1.628	1.838	2.074	2.340	2.639	49
50	1.453	1.645	1.861	2.105	2.381	2.692	50

n	2½%	3%	3½%	4%	4½%	5%	n
1	1.025	1.030	1.035	1.040	1.045	1.050	1
2	1.051	1.061	1.071	1.082	1.092	1.103	2
3	1.077	1.093	1.109	1.125	1.141	1.158	3
4	1.104	1.126	1.148	1.170	1.193	1.216	4
5	1.131	1.159	1.188	1.217	1.246	1.276	5
6	1.160	1.194	1.229	1.265	1.302	1.340	6
7	1.189	1.230	1.272	1.316	1.361	1.407	7
8	1.218	1.267	1.317	1.369	1.422	1.478	8
9	1.249	1.305	1.363	1.423	1.486	1.551	9
10	1.280	1.344	1.411	1.480	1.553	1.629	10
11	1.312	1.384	1.460	1.540	1.623	1.710	11
12	1.345	1.426	1.511	1.601	1.696	1.796	12
13	1.379	1.469	1.564	1.665	1.772	1.886	13
14	1.413	1.513	1.619	1.732	1.852	1.980	14
15	1.448	1.558	1.675	1.801	1.935	2.079	15
16	1.485	1.605	1.734	1.873	2.022	2.183	16
17	1.522	1.653	1.795	1.948	2.113	2.292	17
18	1.560	1.702	1.858	2.026	2.209	2.407	18
19	1.599	1.754	1.923	2.107	2.308	2.527	19
20	1.639	1.806	1.990	2.191	2.412	2.653	20
21	1.680	1.860	2.059	2.279	2.520	2.786	21
22	1.722	1.916	2.132	2.370	2.634	2.925	22
23	1.765	1.974	2.206	2.465	2.752	3.072	23
24	1.809	2.033	2.283	2.563	2.876	3.225	24
25	1.854	2.094	2.363	2.666	3.005	3.386	25
26	1.900	2.157	2.446	2.773	3.141	3.556	26
27	1.948	2.221	2.532	2.883	3.282	3.734	27
28	1.997	2.288	2.620	2.999	3.430	3.920	28
29	2.046	2.357	2.712	3.119	3.584	4.116	29
30	2.098	2.427	2.807	3.243	3.745	4.322	30
31	2.150	2.500	2.905	3.373	3.914	4.538	31
32	2.204	2.575	3.007	3.508	4.090	4.765	32
33	2.259	2.652	3.112	3.648	4.274	5.003	33
34	2.315	2.732	3.221	3.794	4.466	5.253	34
35	2.373	2.814	3.334	3.946	4.667	5.516	35
36	2.433	2.898	3.450	4.104	4.877	5.792	36
37	2.493	2.985	3.571	4.268	5.097	6.081	37
38	2.556	3.075	3.696	4.439	5.326	6.386	38
39	2.620	3.167	3.825	4.616	5.566	6.705	39
40	2.685	3.262	3.959	4.801	5.816	7.040	40
41	2.752	3.360	4.098	4.993	6.078	7.392	41
42	2.821	3.461	4.241	5.193	6.352	7.762	42
43	2.892	3.565	4.390	5.401	6.637	8.150	43
44	2.964	3.672	4.543	5.617	6.936	8.557	44
45	3.038	3.782	4.702	5.841	7.248	8.985	45
46	3.114	3.895	4.867	6.075	7.574	9.434	46
47	3.192	4.012	5.037	6.318	7.915	9.906	47
48	3.272	4.132	5.214	6.571	8.272	10.401	48
49	3.353	4.256	5.396	6.833	8.644	10.921	49
50	3.437	4.384	5.585	7.107	9.033	11.467	50

n	5½%	6%	6½%	7%	7½%	8%	n
1	1.055	1.060	1.065	1.070	1.075	1.080	1
2	1.113	1.124	1.134	1.145	1.156	1.166	2
3	1.174	1.191	1.208	1.225	1.242	1.260	3
4	1.239	1.263	1.287	1.311	1.336	1.361	4
5	1.307	1.338	1.370	1.403	1.436	1.469	5
6	1.378	1.419	1.459	1.501	1.543	1.587	6
7	1.455	1.504	1.554	1.606	1.659	1.714	7
8	1.535	1.594	1.655	1.718	1.784	1.851	8
9	1.619	1.690	1.763	1.839	1.917	1.999	9
10	1.708	1.791	1.877	1.967	2.061	2.159	10
11	1.802	1.898	1.999	2.105	2.216	2.332	11
12	1.901	2.012	2.129	2.252	2.382	2.518	12
13	2.006	2.133	2.268	2.410	2.560	2.720	13
14	2.116	2.261	2.415	2.579	2.752	2.937	14
15	2.233	2.397	2.572	2.759	2.959	3.172	15
16	2.355	2.540	2.739	2.952	3.181	3.426	16
17	2.485	2.693	2.917	3.159	3.419	3.700	17
18	2.621	2.854	3.107	3.380	3.676	3.996	18
19	2.766	3.026	3.309	3.617	3.952	4.316	19
20	2.918	3.207	3.524	3.870	4.248	4.661	20
21	3.078	3.400	3.753	4.141	4.567	5.034	21
22	3.248	3.604	3.997	4.430	4.909	5.437	22
23	3.426	3.820	4.256	4.741	5.277	5.872	23
24	3.615	4.049	4.533	5.072	5.673	6.341	24
25	3.813	4.292	4.828	5.427	6.098	6.849	25
26	4.023	4.549	5.142	5.807	6.556	7.396	26
27	4.244	4.822	5.476	6.214	7.047	7.988	27
28	4.478	5.112	5.832	6.649	7.576	8.627	28
29	4.724	5.418	6.211	7.114	8.144	9.317	29
30	4.984	5.744	6.614	7.612	8.755	10.063	30
31	5.258	6.088	7.044	8.145	9.412	10.868	31
32	5.547	6.453	7.502	8.715	10.118	11.737	32
33	5.852	6.841	7.990	9.325	10.876	12.676	33
34	6.174	7.251	8.509	9.978	11.692	13.690	34
35	6.514	7.686	9.062	10.677	12.569	14.785	35
36	6.872	8.147	9.651	11.424	13.512	15.968	36
37	7.250	8.636	10.279	12.224	14.525	17.246	37
38	7.649	9.154	10.947	13.079	15.614	18.625	38
39	8.070	9.704	11.658	13.995	16.785	20.115	39
40	8.513	10.286	12.416	14.975	18.044	21.725	40
41	8.982	10.903	13.223	16.023	19.398	23.463	41
42	9.476	11.557	14.083	17.144	20.852	25.340	42
43	9.997	12.251	14.998	18.344	22.416	27.367	43
44	10.547	12.986	15.973	19.629	24.098	29.556	44
45	11.127	13.765	17.011	21.003	25.905	31.921	45
46	11.739	14.591	18.117	22.473	27.848	34.474	46
47	12.384	15.466	19.294	24.046	29.936	37.232	47
48	13.065	16.394	20.549	25.729	32.182	40.211	48
49	13.784	17.378	21.884	27.530	34.595	43.427	49
50	14.542	18.420	23.307	29.457	37.190	46.902	50

n	9%	10%	11%	12%	13%	14%	n
1	1.090	1.100	1.110	1.120	1.130	1.140	1
2	1.188	1.210	1.232	1.254	1.277	1.300	2
3	1.295	1.331	1.368	1.405	1.443	1.482	3
4	1.412	1.464	1.518	1.574	1.631	1.689	4
5	1.539	1.611	1.685	1.762	1.842	1.925	5
6	1.677	1.772	1.870	1.974	2.082	2.195	6
7	1.828	1.949	2.076	2.211	2.353	2.502	7
8	1.993	2.144	2.305	2.476	2.658	2.853	8
9	2.172	2.358	2.558	2.773	3.004	3.252	9
10	2.367	2.594	2.839	3.106	3.395	3.707	10
11	2.580	2.853	3.152	3.479	3.836	4.226	11
12	2.813	3.138	3.499	3.896	4.335	4.818	12
13	3.066	3.452	3.883	4.364	4.898	5.492	13
14	3.342	3.798	4.310	4.887	5.535	6.261	14
15	3.643	4.177	4.785	5.474	6.254	7.138	15
16	3.970	4.595	5.311	6.130	7.067	8.137	16
17	4.328	5.055	5.895	6.866	7.986	9.277	17
18	4.717	5.560	6.544	7.690	9.024	10.575	18
19	5.142	6.116	7.263	8.613	10.197	12.056	19
20	5.604	6.728	8.062	9.646	11.523	13.743	20
21	6.109	7.400	8.949	10.804	13.021	15.668	21
22	6.659	8.140	9.934	12.100	14.714	17.861	22
23	7.258	8.954	11.026	13.552	16.627	20.362	23
24	7.911	9.850	12.239	15.179	18.788	23.212	24
25	8.623	10.835	13.585	17.000	21.231	26.462	25
26	9.399	11.918	15.080	19.040	23.991	30.167	26
27	10.245	13.110	16.739	21.325	27.109	34.390	27
28	11.167	14.421	18.580	23.884	30.633	39.204	28
29	12.172	15.863	20.624	26.750	34.616	44.693	29
30	13.268	17.449	22.892	29.960	39.116	50.950	30
31	14.462	19.194	25.410	33.555	44.201	58.083	31
32	15.763	21.114	28.206	37.582	49.947	66.215	32
33	17.182	23.225	31.308	42.092	56.440	75.485	33
34	18.728	25.548	34.752	47.143	63.777	86.053	34
35	20.414	28.102	38.575	52.800	72.069	98.100	35
36	22.251	30.913	42.818	59.136	81.437	111.83	36
37	24.254	34.004	47.528	66.232	92.024	127.49	37
38	26.437	37.404	52.756	74.180	103.99	145.34	38
39	28.816	41.145	58.559	83.081	117.51	165.69	39
40	31.409	45.259	65.001	93.051	132.78	188.88	40
41	34.236	49.785	72.151	104.22	150.04	215.33	41
42	37.318	54.764	80.088	116.72	169.55	245.47	42
43	40.676	60.240	88.897	130.73	191.59	279.84	43
44	44.337	66.264	98.676	146.42	216.50	319.02	44
45	48.327	72.891	109.53	163.99	244.64	363.68	45
46	52.677	80.180	121.58	183.67	276.44	414.59	46
47	57.418	88.198	134.95	205.71	312.38	472.64	47
48	62.585	97.017	149.80	230.39	352.99	538.81	48
49	68.218	106.72	166.27	258.04	398.88	614.24	49
50	74.358	117.39	184.56	289.00	450.74	700.23	50

n	15%	16%	17%	18%	19%	20%	n
1	1.150	1.160	1.170	1.180	1.190	1.200	1
2	1.323	1.346	1.369	1.392	1.416	1.440	2
3	1.521	1.561	1.602	1.643	1.685	1.728	3
4	1.749	1.811	1.874	1.939	2.005	2.074	4
5	2.011	2.100	2.192	2.288	2.386	2.488	5
6	2.313	2.436	2.565	2.700	2.840	2.986	6
7	2.660	2.826	3.001	3.186	3.379	3.583	7
8	3.059	3.278	3.512	3.759	4.021	4.300	8
9	3.518	3.803	4.108	4.436	4.785	5.160	9
10	4.046	4.411	4.807	5.234	5.695	6.192	10
11	4.652	5.117	5.624	6.176	6.777	7.430	11
12	5.350	5.936	6.580	7.288	8.064	8.916	12
13	6.153	6.886	7.699	8.599	9.596	10.699	13
14	7.076	7.988	9.008	10.147	11.420	12.839	14
15	8.137	9.266	10.539	11.974	13.590	15.407	15
16	9.358	10.748	12.330	14.129	16.172	18.488	16
17	10.761	12.468	14.426	16.672	19.244	22.186	17
18	12.375	14.463	16.879	19.673	22.901	26.623	18
19	14.232	16.777	19.748	23.214	27.252	31.948	19
20	16.367	19.461	23.106	27.393	32.429	38.338	20
21	18.822	22.574	27.034	32.324	38.591	46.005	21
22	21.645	26.186	31.629	38.142	45.923	55.206	22
23	24.891	30.376	37.006	45.008	54.649	66.247	23
24	28.625	35.236	43.297	53.109	65.032	79.497	24
25	32.919	40.874	50.658	62.669	77.388	95.396	25
26	37.857	47.414	59.270	73.949	92.092	114.48	26
27	43.535	55.000	69.345	87.260	109.59	137.37	27
28	50.066	63.800	81.134	102.97	130.41	164.84	28
29	57.575	74.009	94.927	121.50	155.19	197.81	29
30	66.212	85.850	111.06	143.37	184.68	237.38	30
31	76.144	99.586	129.95	169.18	219.76	284.85	31
32	87.565	115.52	152.04	199.63	261.52	341.82	32
33	100.70	134.00	177.88	235.56	311.21	410.19	33
34	115.80	155.44	208.12	277.96	370.34	492.22	34
35	133.18	180.31	243.50	328.00	440.70	590.67	35
36	153.15	209.16	284.90	387.04	524.43	708.80	36
37	176.12	242.63	333.33	456.70	624.08	850.56	37
38	202.54	281.45	390.00	538.91	742.65	1020.7	38
39	232.92	326.48	456.30	635.91	883.75	1224.8	39
40	267.86	378.72	533.87	750.38	1051.7	1469.8	40
41	308.04	439.32	624.63	885.45	1251.5	1763.7	41
42	354.25	509.61	730.81	1044.8	1489.3	2116.5	42
43	407.39	591.14	855.05	1232.9	1772.2	2539.8	43
44	468.50	685.73	1000.4	1454.8	2109.0	3047.7	44
45	538.77	795.44	1170.5	1716.7	2509.7	3657.3	45
46	619.58	922.72	1369.5	2025.7	2986.5	4388.7	46
47	712.52	1070.3	1602.3	2390.3	3553.9	5266.5	47
48	819.40	1241.6	1874.7	2820.6	4229.2	6319.7	48
49	942.31	1440.3	2193.3	3328.3	5032.7	7583.7	49
50	1083.7	1670.7	2566.2	3927.4	5988.9	9100.4	50

TABLE 2: The Present Value of \$1 (The Present Value of \$1 to Be Received or Spent in the Future): $PV = S \times n]\,i$

n	¾%	1%	1¼%	1½%	1¾%	2%	n
1	0.993	0.990	0.988	0.985	0.983	0.980	1
2	0.985	0.980	0.976	0.971	0.966	0.961	2
3	0.978	0.971	0.963	0.956	0.949	0.942	3
4	0.971	0.961	0.952	0.942	0.933	0.924	4
5	0.963	0.952	0.940	0.928	0.917	0.906	5
6	0.956	0.942	0.928	0.915	0.901	0.888	6
7	0.949	0.933	0.917	0.901	0.886	0.871	7
8	0.942	0.924	0.905	0.888	0.870	0.854	8
9	0.935	0.914	0.894	0.875	0.855	0.837	9
10	0.928	0.905	0.883	0.862	0.841	0.820	10
11	0.921	0.896	0.872	0.849	0.826	0.804	11
12	0.914	0.888	0.862	0.836	0.812	0.789	12
13	0.907	0.879	0.851	0.824	0.798	0.773	13
14	0.901	0.870	0.840	0.812	0.784	0.758	14
15	0.894	0.861	0.830	0.800	0.771	0.743	15
16	0.887	0.853	0.820	0.788	0.758	0.729	16
17	0.881	0.844	0.810	0.776	0.745	0.714	17
18	0.874	0.836	0.800	0.765	0.732	0.700	18
19	0.868	0.828	0.790	0.754	0.719	0.686	19
20	0.861	0.820	0.780	0.743	0.707	0.673	20
21	0.855	0.811	0.770	0.732	0.695	0.660	21
22	0.848	0.803	0.761	0.721	0.683	0.647	22
23	0.842	0.795	0.752	0.710	0.671	0.634	23
24	0.836	0.788	0.742	0.700	0.659	0.622	24
25	0.830	0.780	0.733	0.689	0.648	0.610	25
26	0.823	0.772	0.724	0.679	0.637	0.598	26
27	0.817	0.764	0.715	0.669	0.626	0.586	27
28	0.811	0.757	0.706	0.659	0.615	0.574	28
29	0.805	0.749	0.698	0.649	0.605	0.563	29
30	0.799	0.742	0.689	0.640	0.594	0.552	30
31	0.793	0.735	0.680	0.630	0.584	0.541	31
32	0.787	0.727	0.672	0.621	0.574	0.531	32
33	0.782	0.720	0.664	0.612	0.564	0.520	33
34	0.776	0.713	0.656	0.603	0.554	0.510	34
35	0.770	0.706	0.647	0.594	0.545	0.500	35
36	0.764	0.699	0.639	0.585	0.536	0.490	36
37	0.759	0.692	0.632	0.576	0.526	0.481	37
38	0.753	0.685	0.624	0.568	0.517	0.471	38
39	0.747	0.678	0.616	0.560	0.508	0.462	39
40	0.742	0.672	0.608	0.551	0.500	0.453	40
41	0.736	0.665	0.601	0.543	0.491	0.444	41
42	0.731	0.658	0.594	0.535	0.483	0.435	42
43	0.725	0.652	0.586	0.527	0.474	0.427	43
44	0.720	0.646	0.579	0.519	0.466	0.418	44
45	0.715	0.639	0.572	0.512	0.458	0.410	45
46	0.709	0.633	0.565	0.504	0.450	0.402	46
47	0.704	0.627	0.558	0.497	0.443	0.394	47
48	0.699	0.620	0.551	0.489	0.435	0.387	48
49	0.693	0.614	0.544	0.482	0.427	0.379	49
50	0.688	0.608	0.537	0.475	0.420	0.372	50

n	2½%	3%	3½%	4%	4½%	5%	n
1	0.976	0.971	0.966	0.962	0.957	0.952	1
2	0.952	0.943	0.934	0.925	0.916	0.907	2
3	0.929	0.915	0.902	0.889	0.876	0.864	3
4	0.906	0.889	0.871	0.855	0.839	0.823	4
5	0.884	0.863	0.842	0.822	0.803	0.784	5
6	0.862	0.838	0.814	0.790	0.768	0.746	6
7	0.841	0.813	0.786	0.760	0.735	0.711	7
8	0.821	0.789	0.759	0.731	0.703	0.677	8
9	0.801	0.766	0.734	0.703	0.673	0.645	9
10	0.781	0.744	0.709	0.676	0.644	0.614	10
11	0.762	0.722	0.685	0.650	0.616	0.585	11
12	0.744	0.701	0.662	0.625	0.590	0.557	12
13	0.725	0.681	0.639	0.601	0.564	0.530	13
14	0.708	0.661	0.618	0.578	0.540	0.505	14
15	0.691	0.642	0.597	0.555	0.517	0.481	15
16	0.674	0.623	0.577	0.534	0.495	0.458	16
17	0.657	0.605	0.557	0.513	0.473	0.436	17
18	0.641	0.587	0.538	0.494	0.453	0.416	18
19	0.626	0.570	0.520	0.475	0.433	0.396	19
20	0.610	0.554	0.503	0.456	0.415	0.377	20
21	0.595	0.538	0.486	0.439	0.397	0.359	21
22	0.581	0.522	0.469	0.422	0.380	0.342	22
23	0.567	0.507	0.453	0.406	0.363	0.326	23
24	0.553	0.492	0.438	0.390	0.348	0.310	24
25	0.539	0.478	0.423	0.375	0.333	0.295	25
26	0.526	0.464	0.409	0.361	0.318	0.281	26
27	0.513	0.450	0.395	0.347	0.305	0.268	27
28	0.501	0.437	0.382	0.334	0.292	0.255	28
29	0.489	0.424	0.369	0.321	0.279	0.243	29
30	0.477	0.412	0.356	0.308	0.267	0.231	30
31	0.465	0.400	0.344	0.297	0.256	0.220	31
32	0.454	0.388	0.333	0.285	0.245	0.210	32
33	0.443	0.377	0.321	0.274	0.234	0.200	33
34	0.432	0.366	0.311	0.264	0.224	0.190	34
35	0.421	0.355	0.300	0.253	0.214	0.181	35
36	0.411	0.345	0.290	0.244	0.205	0.173	36
37	0.401	0.335	0.280	0.234	0.196	0.164	37
38	0.391	0.325	0.271	0.225	0.188	0.157	38
39	0.382	0.316	0.261	0.217	0.180	0.149	39
40	0.372	0.307	0.253	0.208	0.172	0.142	40
41	0.363	0.298	0.244	0.200	0.165	0.135	41
42	0.355	0.289	0.236	0.193	0.157	0.129	42
43	0.346	0.281	0.228	0.185	0.151	0.123	43
44	0.337	0.272	0.220	0.178	0.144	0.117	44
45	0.329	0.264	0.213	0.171	0.138	0.111	45
46	0.321	0.257	0.206	0.165	0.132	0.106	46
47	0.313	0.249	0.199	0.158	0.126	0.101	47
48	0.306	0.242	0.192	0.152	0.121	0.096	48
49	0.298	0.235	0.185	0.146	0.116	0.092	49
50	0.291	0.228	0.179	0.141	0.111	0.087	50

n	5½%	6%	6½%	7%	7½%	8%	n
1	0.948	0.943	0.939	0.935	0.930	0.926	1
2	0.899	0.890	0.882	0.873	0.865	0.857	2
3	0.852	0.840	0.828	0.816	0.805	0.794	3
4	0.807	0.792	0.777	0.763	0.749	0.735	4
5	0.765	0.747	0.730	0.713	0.697	0.681	5
6	0.725	0.705	0.685	0.666	0.648	0.630	6
7	0.687	0.665	0.644	0.623	0.603	0.584	7
8	0.652	0.627	0.604	0.582	0.561	0.540	8
9	0.618	0.592	0.567	0.544	0.522	0.500	9
10	0.585	0.558	0.533	0.508	0.485	0.463	10
11	0.555	0.527	0.500	0.475	0.451	0.429	11
12	0.526	0.497	0.470	0.444	0.420	0.397	12
13	0.499	0.469	0.441	0.415	0.391	0.368	13
14	0.473	0.442	0.414	0.388	0.363	0.341	14
15	0.448	0.417	0.389	0.363	0.338	0.315	15
16	0.425	0.394	0.365	0.339	0.314	0.292	16
17	0.403	0.371	0.343	0.317	0.293	0.270	17
18	0.382	0.350	0.322	0.296	0.272	0.250	18
19	0.362	0.331	0.302	0.277	0.253	0.232	19
20	0.343	0.312	0.284	0.258	0.235	0.215	20
21	0.325	0.294	0.267	0.242	0.219	0.199	21
22	0.308	0.278	0.250	0.226	0.204	0.184	22
23	0.292	0.262	0.235	0.211	0.190	0.170	23
24	0.277	0.247	0.221	0.197	0.176	0.158	24
25	0.262	0.233	0.207	0.184	0.164	0.146	25
26	0.249	0.220	0.195	0.172	0.153	0.135	26
27	0.236	0.207	0.183	0.161	0.142	0.125	27
28	0.223	0.196	0.172	0.150	0.132	0.116	28
29	0.212	0.185	0.161	0.141	0.123	0.107	29
30	0.201	0.174	0.151	0.131	0.114	0.099	30
31	0.190	0.164	0.142	0.123	0.106	0.092	31
32	0.180	0.155	0.133	0.115	0.099	0.085	32
33	0.171	0.146	0.125	0.107	0.092	0.079	33
34	0.162	0.138	0.118	0.100	0.086	0.073	34
35	0.154	0.130	0.110	0.094	0.080	0.068	35
36	0.146	0.123	0.104	0.088	0.074	0.063	36
37	0.138	0.116	0.097	0.082	0.069	0.058	37
38	0.131	0.109	0.091	0.077	0.064	0.054	38
39	0.124	0.103	0.086	0.071	0.060	0.050	39
40	0.118	0.097	0.081	0.067	0.055	0.046	40
41	0.111	0.092	0.076	0.062	0.052	0.043	41
42	0.106	0.087	0.071	0.058	0.048	0.040	42
43	0.100	0.082	0.067	0.055	0.045	0.037	43
44	0.095	0.077	0.063	0.051	0.042	0.034	44
45	0.090	0.073	0.059	0.048	0.039	0.031	45
46	0.085	0.069	0.055	0.045	0.036	0.029	46
47	0.081	0.065	0.052	0.042	0.033	0.027	47
48	0.077	0.061	0.049	0.039	0.031	0.025	48
49	0.073	0.058	0.046	0.036	0.029	0.023	49
50	0.069	0.054	0.043	0.034	0.027	0.021	50

n	9%	10%	11%	12%	13%	14%	n
1	0.917	0.909	0.901	0.893	0.885	0.877	1
2	0.842	0.827	0.812	0.797	0.783	0.770	2
3	0.772	0.751	0.731	0.712	0.693	0.675	3
4	0.708	0.683	0.659	0.636	0.613	0.592	4
5	0.650	0.621	0.594	0.567	0.542	0.519	5
6	0.596	0.565	0.535	0.507	0.480	0.456	6
7	0.547	0.513	0.482	0.452	0.425	0.400	7
8	0.502	0.467	0.434	0.404	0.376	0.351	8
9	0.460	0.424	0.391	0.361	0.333	0.308	9
10	0.422	0.386	0.352	0.322	0.295	0.270	10
11	0.388	0.351	0.317	0.288	0.261	0.237	11
12	0.356	0.319	0.286	0.257	0.231	0.208	12
13	0.326	0.290	0.258	0.229	0.204	0.182	13
14	0.299	0.263	0.232	0.205	0.181	0.160	14
15	0.275	0.239	0.209	0.183	0.160	0.140	15
16	0.252	0.218	0.188	0.163	0.142	0.123	16
17	0.231	0.198	0.170	0.146	0.125	0.108	17
18	0.212	0.180	0.153	0.130	0.111	0.095	18
19	0.195	0.164	0.138	0.116	0.098	0.083	19
20	0.178	0.149	0.124	0.104	0.087	0.073	20
21	0.164	0.135	0.112	0.093	0.077	0.064	21
22	0.150	0.123	0.101	0.083	0.068	0.056	22
23	0.138	0.112	0.091	0.074	0.060	0.049	23
24	0.126	0.102	0.082	0.066	0.053	0.043	24
25	0.116	0.092	0.074	0.059	0.047	0.038	25
26	0.106	0.084	0.066	0.053	0.042	0.033	26
27	0.098	0.076	0.060	0.047	0.037	0.029	27
28	0.090	0.069	0.054	0.042	0.033	0.026	28
29	0.082	0.063	0.049	0.037	0.029	0.022	29
30	0.075	0.057	0.044	0.033	0.026	0.020	30
31	0.069	0.052	0.039	0.030	0.023	0.017	31
32	0.063	0.047	0.036	0.027	0.020	0.015	32
33	0.058	0.043	0.032	0.024	0.018	0.013	33
34	0.053	0.039	0.029	0.021	0.016	0.012	34
35	0.049	0.036	0.026	0.019	0.014	0.010	35
36	0.045	0.032	0.023	0.017	0.012	0.009	36
37	0.041	0.029	0.021	0.015	0.011	0.008	37
38	0.038	0.027	0.019	0.014	0.010	0.007	38
39	0.035	0.024	0.017	0.012	0.009	0.006	39
40	0.032	0.022	0.015	0.011	0.008	0.005	40
41	0.029	0.020	0.014	0.010	0.007	0.005	41
42	0.027	0.018	0.013	0.009	0.006	0.004	42
43	0.025	0.017	0.011	0.008	0.005	0.004	43
44	0.023	0.015	0.010	0.007	0.005	0.003	44
45	0.021	0.014	0.009	0.006	0.004	0.003	45
46	0.019	0.013	0.008	0.006	0.004	0.002	46
47	0.017	0.011	0.007	0.005	0.003	0.002	47
48	0.016	0.010	0.007	0.004	0.003	0.002	48
49	0.015	0.009	0.006	0.004	0.003	0.002	49
50	0.014	0.009	0.005	0.004	0.002	0.001	50

n	15%	16%	17%	18%	19%	20%	n
1	0.870	0.862	0.855	0.848	0.840	0.833	1
2	0.756	0.743	0.731	0.718	0.706	0.694	2
3	0.658	0.641	0.624	0.609	0.593	0.579	3
4	0.572	0.552	0.534	0.516	0.499	0.482	4
5	0.497	0.476	0.456	0.437	0.419	0.402	5
6	0.432	0.410	0.390	0.370	0.352	0.335	6
7	0.376	0.354	0.333	0.314	0.296	0.279	7
8	0.327	0.305	0.285	0.266	0.249	0.233	8
9	0.284	0.263	0.243	0.226	0.209	0.194	9
10	0.247	0.227	0.208	0.191	0.176	0.162	10
11	0.215	0.195	0.178	0.162	0.148	0.135	11
12	0.187	0.169	0.152	0.137	0.124	0.112	12
13	0.163	0.145	0.130	0.116	0.104	0.094	13
14	0.141	0.125	0.111	0.099	0.088	0.078	14
15	0.123	0.108	0.095	0.084	0.074	0.065	15
16	0.107	0.093	0.081	0.071	0.062	0.054	16
17	0.093	0.080	0.069	0.060	0.052	0.045	17
18	0.081	0.069	0.059	0.051	0.044	0.038	18
19	0.070	0.060	0.051	0.043	0.037	0.031	19
20	0.061	0.051	0.043	0.037	0.031	0.026	20
21	0.053	0.044	0.037	0.031	0.026	0.022	21
22	0.046	0.038	0.032	0.026	0.022	0.018	22
23	0.040	0.033	0.027	0.022	0.018	0.015	23
24	0.035	0.028	0.023	0.019	0.015	0.013	24
25	0.030	0.025	0.020	0.016	0.013	0.011	25
26	0.026	0.021	0.017	0.014	0.011	0.009	26
27	0.023	0.018	0.014	0.012	0.009	0.007	27
28	0.020	0.016	0.012	0.010	0.008	0.006	28
29	0.017	0.014	0.011	0.008	0.006	0.005	29
30	0.015	0.012	0.009	0.007	0.005	0.004	30
31	0.013	0.010	0.008	0.006	0.005	0.004	31
32	0.011	0.009	0.007	0.005	0.004	0.003	32
33	0.010	0.008	0.006	0.004	0.003	0.002	33
34	0.009	0.006	0.005	0.004	0.003	0.002	34
35	0.008	0.006	0.004	0.003	0.002	0.002	35
36	0.007	0.005	0.004	0.003	0.002	0.001	36
37	0.006	0.004	0.003	0.002	0.002	0.001	37
38	0.005	0.004	0.003	0.002	0.001	0.001	38
39	0.004	0.003	0.002	0.002	0.001	0.001	39
40	0.004	0.003	0.002	0.001	0.001	0.001	40
41	0.003	0.002	0.002	0.001	0.001	0.001	41
42	0.003	0.002	0.001	0.001	0.001	0.001	42
43	0.003	0.002	0.001	0.001	0.001	0.000	43
44	0.002	0.002	0.001	0.001	0.001	0.000	44
45	0.002	0.001	0.001	0.001	0.000	0.000	45
46	0.002	0.001	0.001	0.001	0.000	0.000	46
47	0.001	0.001	0.001	0.000	0.000	0.000	47
48	0.001	0.001	0.001	0.000	0.000	0.000	48
49	0.001	0.001	0.001	0.000	0.000	0.000	49
50	0.001	0.001	0.000	0.000	0.000	0.000	50

TABLE 3: The Amount of an Annuity of $1 (The Value [or Amount] to Which $1 Paid in Per Period Starting Now Adds Up If It Is Invested at Compound Interest): $V_a = S_a \times n]\,i$

n	¾%	1%	1¼%	1½%	1¾%	2%	n
1	1.000	1.000	1.000	1.000	1.000	1.000	1
2	2.008	2.010	2.013	2.015	2.018	2.020	2
3	3.023	3.030	3.038	3.045	3.053	3.060	3
4	4.045	4.060	4.076	4.091	4.106	4.122	4
5	5.076	5.101	5.127	5.152	5.178	5.204	5
6	6.114	6.152	6.191	6.230	6.269	6.308	6
7	7.160	7.214	7.268	7.323	7.378	7.434	7
8	8.213	8.286	8.359	8.433	8.508	8.583	8
9	9.275	9.369	9.463	9.559	9.656	9.755	9
10	10.344	10.462	10.582	10.703	10.825	10.950	10
11	11.422	11.567	11.714	11.863	12.015	12.169	11
12	12.508	12.683	12.860	13.041	13.225	13.412	12
13	13.601	13.809	14.021	14.237	14.457	14.680	13
14	14.703	14.947	15.196	15.450	15.710	15.974	14
15	15.814	16.097	16.386	16.682	16.985	17.293	15
16	16.932	17.258	17.591	17.932	18.282	18.639	16
17	18.059	18.430	18.811	19.201	19.602	20.012	17
18	19.195	19.615	20.046	20.489	20.945	21.412	18
19	20.339	20.811	21.297	21.797	22.311	22.841	19
20	21.491	22.019	22.563	23.124	23.702	24.297	20
21	22.652	23.239	23.845	24.471	25.116	25.783	21
22	23.822	24.472	25.143	25.838	26.556	27.299	22
23	25.001	25.716	26.457	27.225	28.021	28.845	23
24	26.189	26.974	27.788	28.634	29.511	30.422	24
25	27.385	28.243	29.135	30.063	31.028	32.030	25
26	28.590	29.526	30.500	31.514	32.570	33.671	26
27	29.805	30.821	31.881	32.987	34.140	35.344	27
28	31.028	32.129	33.279	34.482	35.738	37.051	28
29	32.261	33.450	34.695	35.999	37.363	38.792	29
30	33.503	34.785	36.129	37.539	39.017	40.568	30
31	34.754	36.133	37.581	39.102	40.700	42.379	31
32	36.015	37.494	39.050	40.688	42.412	44.227	32
33	37.285	38.869	40.539	42.299	44.154	46.112	33
34	38.565	40.258	42.045	43.933	45.927	48.034	34
35	39.854	41.660	43.571	45.592	47.731	49.995	35
36	41.153	43.077	45.116	47.276	49.566	51.994	36
37	42.461	44.508	46.680	48.985	51.434	54.034	37
38	43.780	45.953	48.293	50.720	53.334	56.115	38
39	45.108	47.412	49.886	52.481	55.267	58.237	39
40	46.447	48.886	51.490	54.268	57.234	60.402	40
41	47.795	50.375	53.133	56.082	59.236	62.610	41
42	49.153	51.879	54.797	57.923	61.272	64.862	42
43	50.522	53.398	56.482	59.792	63.345	67.160	43
44	51.901	54.932	58.188	61.689	65.453	69.503	44
45	53.290	56.481	59.916	63.614	67.599	71.893	45
46	54.690	58.046	61.665	65.568	69.782	74.331	46
47	56.100	59.626	63.436	67.552	72.003	76.817	47
48	57.521	61.223	65.228	69.565	74.263	79.354	48
49	58.952	62.835	67.044	71.609	76.562	81.941	49
50	60.394	64.463	68.882	73.683	78.902	84.579	50

n	2½%	3%	3½%	4%	4½%	5%	n
1	1.000	1.000	1.000	1.000	1.000	1.000	1
2	2.025	2.030	2.035	2.040	2.045	2.050	2
3	3.076	3.091	3.106	3.122	3.137	3.153	3
4	4.153	4.184	4.215	4.247	4.278	4.310	4
5	5.256	5.309	5.363	5.416	5.471	5.526	5
6	6.388	6.468	6.550	6.633	6.717	6.802	6
7	7.547	7.663	7.779	7.898	8.019	8.142	7
8	8.736	8.892	9.052	9.214	9.380	9.549	8
9	9.955	10.159	10.369	10.583	10.802	11.027	9
10	11.203	11.464	11.731	12.006	12.288	12.578	10
11	12.484	12.808	12.142	13.486	13.841	14.207	11
12	13.796	14.192	14.602	15.026	15.464	15.917	12
13	15.140	15.618	16.113	16.627	17.160	17.713	13
14	16.519	17.086	17.677	18.292	18.932	19.599	14
15	17.932	18.599	19.296	20.024	20.784	21.579	15
16	19.380	20.157	20.971	21.825	22.719	23.658	16
17	20.865	21.762	22.705	23.698	24.742	25.840	17
18	22.386	23.414	24.500	25.645	26.855	28.132	18
19	23.946	25.117	26.357	27.671	29.064	30.539	19
20	25.545	26.870	28.280	29.778	31.371	33.066	20
21	27.183	28.677	30.270	31.969	33.783	35.719	21
22	28.863	30.537	32.329	34.248	36.303	38.505	22
23	30.584	32.453	34.460	36.618	38.937	41.431	23
24	32.349	34.427	36.667	39.083	41.689	44.502	24
25	34.158	36.459	38.950	41.646	44.565	47.727	25
26	36.012	38.553	41.313	44.312	47.571	51.114	26
27	37.912	40.710	43.759	47.084	50.711	54.669	27
28	39.860	42.931	46.290	49.968	53.993	58.403	28
29	41.856	45.219	48.911	52.966	57.423	62.323	29
30	43.903	47.575	51.623	56.085	61.007	66.439	30
31	46.000	50.003	54.430	59.328	64.752	70.761	31
32	48.150	52.503	57.335	62.702	68.666	75.299	32
33	50.354	55.078	60.341	66.210	72.756	80.064	33
34	52.613	57.730	63.453	69.858	77.030	85.067	34
35	54.928	60.462	66.674	73.652	81.497	90.320	35
36	57.301	63.276	70.008	77.598	86.164	95.836	36
37	59.734	66.174	73.458	81.702	91.041	101.628	37
38	62.227	69.160	77.029	85.970	96.138	107.710	38
39	64.783	72.234	80.725	90.409	101.464	114.095	39
40	67.403	75.401	84.550	95.026	107.030	120.800	40
41	70.088	78.663	88.510	99.827	112.847	127.840	41
42	72.840	82.023	92.607	104.820	118.925	135.232	42
43	75.661	85.484	96.849	110.012	125.276	142.993	43
44	78.552	89.048	101.238	115.413	131.914	151.143	44
45	81.516	92.720	105.782	121.029	138.850	159.700	45
46	84.554	96.502	110.484	126.871	146.098	168.685	46
47	87.668	100.397	115.351	132.945	153.673	178.119	47
48	90.860	104.408	120.388	139.263	161.588	188.025	48
49	94.131	108.541	125.602	145.834	169.860	198.427	49
50	97.484	112.797	130.998	152.667	178.503	209.348	50

n	5½%	6%	6½%	7%	7½%	8%	n
1	1.000	1.000	1.000	1.000	1.000	1.000	1
2	2.055	2.060	2.065	2.070	2.075	2.080	2
3	3.168	3.184	3.199	3.215	3.231	3.246	3
4	4.342	4.375	4.407	4.440	4.473	4.506	4
5	5.581	5.637	5.694	5.751	5.808	5.867	5
6	6.888	6.975	7.064	7.153	7.244	7.336	6
7	8.267	8.394	8.523	8.654	8.787	8.923	7
8	9.722	9.898	10.077	10.260	10.446	10.637	8
9	11.256	11.491	11.732	11.978	12.230	12.488	9
10	12.875	13.181	13.494	13.817	14.147	14.487	10
11	14.584	14.972	15.372	15.784	16.208	16.646	11
12	16.386	16.870	17.371	17.889	18.424	18.977	12
13	18.287	18.882	19.500	20.141	20.806	21.495	13
14	20.293	21.015	21.767	22.551	23.366	24.215	14
15	22.409	23.276	24.182	25.129	26.118	27.152	15
16	24.641	25.673	26.754	27.888	29.077	30.324	16
17	26.996	28.213	29.493	30.840	32.258	33.750	17
18	29.481	30.906	32.410	33.999	35.677	37.450	18
19	32.103	33.760	35.517	37.379	39.353	41.446	19
20	34.868	36.786	38.825	40.996	43.305	45.762	20
21	37.786	39.993	42.349	44.865	47.553	50.423	21
22	40.864	43.392	46.102	49.006	52.119	55.457	22
23	44.112	46.996	50.098	53.436	57.028	60.893	23
24	47.538	50.816	54.355	58.177	62.305	66.765	24
25	51.153	54.865	58.888	63.249	67.978	73.106	25
26	54.966	59.156	63.715	68.677	74.076	79.954	26
27	58.989	63.706	68.857	74.484	80.632	87.351	27
28	63.234	68.528	74.333	80.698	87.679	95.339	28
29	67.711	73.640	80.164	87.347	95.255	103.966	29
30	72.436	79.058	86.375	94.461	103.399	113.283	30
31	77.419	84.802	92.989	102.073	112.154	123.346	31
32	82.678	90.890	100.034	110.218	121.566	134.214	32
33	88.225	97.343	107.536	118.933	131.683	145.951	33
34	94.077	104.184	115.526	128.259	142.560	158.627	34
35	100.251	111.435	124.035	138.237	154.252	172.317	35
36	106.765	119.121	133.097	148.914	166.821	187.102	36
37	113.637	127.268	142.748	160.337	180.332	203.070	37
38	120.887	135.904	153.027	172.561	194.857	220.316	38
39	128.536	145.059	163.974	185.640	210.471	238.941	39
40	136.606	154.762	175.632	199.635	227.257	259.057	40
41	145.119	165.048	188.048	214.610	245.301	280.781	41
42	154.101	175.951	201.271	230.632	264.698	304.244	42
43	163.576	187.508	215.354	247.777	285.551	329.583	43
44	173.573	199.758	230.352	266.121	307.967	356.950	44
45	184.119	212.744	246.325	285.749	332.065	386.506	45
46	195.246	226.508	263.336	306.752	357.969	418.426	46
47	206.984	241.099	281.453	329.224	385.817	452.900	47
48	219.368	256.565	300.747	353.270	415.753	490.132	48
49	232.434	272.958	321.296	378.999	447.935	530.343	49
50	246.218	290.336	343.180	406.529	482.530	573.770	50

n	9%	10%	11%	12%	13%	14%	n
1	1.000	1.000	1.000	1.000	1.000	1.000	1
2	2.090	2.100	2.110	2.120	2.130	2.140	2
3	3.278	3.310	3.342	3.374	3.407	3.440	3
4	4.573	4.641	4.710	4.779	4.850	4.921	4
5	5.985	6.105	6.228	6.353	6.480	6.610	5
6	7.523	7.716	7.913	8.115	8.323	8.536	6
7	9.200	9.487	9.783	10.089	10.405	10.731	7
8	11.029	11.436	11.859	12.300	12.757	13.233	8
9	13.021	13.580	14.164	14.776	15.416	16.085	9
10	15.193	15.937	16.722	17.549	18.420	19.337	10
11	17.560	18.531	19.561	20.655	21.814	23.045	11
12	20.141	21.384	22.713	24.133	25.650	27.271	12
13	22.953	24.523	26.212	28.029	29.985	32.089	13
14	26.019	27.975	30.095	32.393	34.883	37.581	14
15	29.361	31.773	34.405	37.280	40.418	43.842	15
16	33.003	35.950	39.190	42.753	46.672	50.980	16
17	36.974	40.545	44.501	48.884	53.739	59.118	17
18	41.301	45.599	50.396	55.750	61.725	68.394	18
19	46.019	51.159	56.940	63.440	70.749	78.969	19
20	51.160	57.275	64.203	72.052	80.947	91.025	20
21	56.765	64.003	72.265	81.699	92.470	104.768	21
22	62.873	71.403	81.214	92.503	105.491	120.436	22
23	69.532	79.543	91.148	104.603	120.205	138.297	23
24	76.790	88.497	102.174	118.155	136.831	158.659	24
25	84.701	98.347	114.413	133.334	155.620	181.871	25
26	93.324	109.182	127.999	150.334	176.850	208.333	26
27	102.723	121.100	143.079	169.374	200.841	238.499	27
28	112.968	134.210	159.817	190.699	227.950	272.889	28
29	124.135	148.631	178.397	214.583	258.583	312.094	29
30	136.308	164.494	199.021	241.333	293.199	356.787	30
31	149.575	181.943	221.913	271.293	332.315	407.737	31
32	164.037	201.138	247.324	304.848	376.516	465.820	32
33	179.800	222.252	275.529	342.429	426.463	532.035	33
34	196.982	245.477	306.837	384.521	482.903	607.520	34
35	215.711	271.024	341.590	431.663	546.681	693.573	35
36	236.125	299.127	380.164	484.463	618.749	791.673	36
37	258.376	330.039	422.982	543.599	700.187	903.507	37
38	282.630	364.043	470.511	609.831	792.211	1031.00	38
39	309.066	401.448	523.267	684.010	896.198	1176.34	39
40	337.882	442.593	581.826	767.091	1013.70	1342.03	40
41	369.292	487.852	646.827	860.142	1146.49	1530.91	41
42	403.528	537.637	718.978	964.359	1296.53	1746.24	42
43	440.846	592.401	799.065	1081.08	1466.08	1991.71	43
44	481.522	652.641	887.963	1211.81	1657.67	2271.55	44
45	525.859	718.905	986.639	1358.23	1874.16	2590.56	45
46	574.186	791.795	1096.17	1522.22	2118.81	2954.24	46
47	626.863	871.975	1217.75	1705.88	2395.25	3368.84	47
48	684.280	960.172	1352.70	1911.59	2707.63	3841.48	48
49	746.866	1057.19	1502.50	2141.98	3060.63	4380.28	49
50	815.084	1163.91	1668.77	2400.02	3459.51	4994.52	50

n	15%	16%	17%	18%	19%	20%	n
1	1.000	1.000	1.000	1.000	1.000	1.000	1
2	2.150	2.160	2.170	2.180	2.190	2.200	2
3	3.473	3.506	3.539	3.572	3.606	3.640	3
4	4.993	5.067	5.141	5.215	5.291	5.368	4
5	6.742	6.877	7.014	7.154	7.297	7.442	5
6	8.754	8.978	9.207	9.442	9.683	9.930	6
7	11.067	11.414	11.772	12.142	12.523	12.916	7
8	13.727	14.240	14.773	15.327	15.902	16.499	8
9	16.786	17.519	18.285	19.086	19.923	20.799	9
10	20.304	21.322	22.393	23.521	24.709	25.959	10
11	24.349	25.733	27.200	28.755	30.404	32.150	11
12	29.002	30.850	32.824	34.931	37.180	39.581	12
13	34.352	36.786	39.404	42.219	45.245	48.497	13
14	40.505	43.672	47.103	50.818	54.841	59.196	14
15	47.580	51.660	56.110	60.965	66.261	72.035	15
16	55.718	60.925	66.649	72.939	79.850	87.442	16
17	65.075	71.673	78.979	87.068	96.022	105.931	17
18	75.836	84.141	93.406	103.740	115.266	128.117	18
19	88.212	98.603	110.285	123.414	138.166	154.740	19
20	102.444	115.380	130.033	146.628	165.418	186.688	20
21	118.810	134.841	153.139	174.021	197.847	225.026	21
22	137.632	157.415	180.172	206.345	236.438	271.031	22
23	159.276	183.601	211.801	244.487	282.362	326.237	23
24	184.168	213.978	248.808	289.494	337.010	392.484	24
25	212.793	249.214	292.105	342.603	402.042	471.981	25
26	245.712	290.088	342.763	405.272	479.431	567.377	26
27	283.569	337.502	402.032	479.221	571.522	681.853	27
28	327.104	392.503	471.378	566.481	681.112	819.223	28
29	377.170	456.303	552.512	669.447	811.523	984.068	29
30	434.745	530.312	647.439	790.948	966.712	1181.88	30
31	500.957	616.162	758.504	934.319	1151.39	1419.26	31
32	577.100	715.747	888.449	1103.50	1371.15	1704.11	32
33	664.666	831.267	1040.49	1303.13	1632.67	2045.93	33
34	765.365	965.270	1218.37	1538.69	1943.88	2456.12	34
35	881.170	1120.71	1426.49	1816.65	2314.21	2948.34	35
36	1014.35	1301.03	1669.99	2144.65	2754.91	3539.01	36
37	1167.50	1510.19	1954.89	2531.69	3279.35	4247.81	37
38	1343.62	1752.82	2288.23	2988.39	3903.42	5098.37	38
39	1546.17	2034.27	2678.22	3527.30	4646.07	6119.05	39
40	1779.09	2360.76	3134.52	4163.21	5529.83	7343.86	40
41	2046.95	2739.48	3668.39	4913.59	6581.50	8813.63	41
42	2355.00	3178.79	4293.02	5799.04	7832.98	10577.4	42
43	2709.25	3688.40	5023.83	6843.86	9322.25	12693.8	43
44	3116.63	4279.55	5878.88	8076.76	11094.5	15233.6	44
45	3585.13	4965.27	6879.29	9531.58	13203.4	18281.3	45
46	4123.90	5760.72	8049.77	11248.3	15713.1	21938.6	46
47	4743.48	6683.43	9419.23	13273.9	18699.6	26327.3	47
48	5456.00	7753.78	11021.5	15664.3	22253.5	31593.7	48
49	6275.41	8995.39	12896.2	18484.8	26482.6	37913.5	49
50	7217.12	10435.6	15089.5	21813.1	31515.3	45497.2	50

**TABLE 4: The Present Value of an Annuity of \$1 (The Present Value of
\$1 to Be Received or Spent Per Period in the Future):** $PV_a = S_a \times n] \, i$

n	¾%	1%	1¼%	1½%	1¾%	2%	n
1	0.993	0.990	0.988	0.985	0.983	0.980	1
2	1.978	1.970	1.963	1.956	1.949	1.942	2
3	2.956	2.941	2.927	2.912	2.898	2.884	3
4	3.926	3.902	3.878	3.854	3.831	3.808	4
5	4.889	4.853	4.818	4.783	4.748	4.714	5
6	5.846	5.796	5.746	5.697	5.649	5.601	6
7	6.795	6.728	6.663	6.598	6.535	6.472	7
8	7.737	7.652	7.568	7.486	7.405	7.326	8
9	8.672	8.566	8.462	8.361	8.261	8.162	9
10	9.600	9.471	9.346	9.222	9.101	8.983	10
11	10.521	10.368	10.218	10.071	9.928	9.787	11
12	11.435	11.255	11.080	10.908	10.740	10.575	12
13	12.342	12.134	11.930	11.732	11.538	11.348	13
14	13.243	13.004	12.771	12.543	12.322	12.106	14
15	14.137	13.865	13.601	13.343	13.093	12.849	15
16	15.024	14.718	14.420	14.131	13.851	13.578	16
17	15.905	15.562	15.230	14.908	14.595	14.292	17
18	16.779	16.398	16.030	15.673	15.327	14.992	18
19	17.647	17.226	16.819	16.426	16.046	15.679	19
20	18.508	18.046	17.599	17.169	16.753	16.351	20
21	19.363	18.857	18.370	17.900	17.448	17.011	21
22	20.211	19.660	19.131	18.621	18.130	17.658	22
23	21.053	20.456	19.882	19.331	18.801	18.292	23
24	21.889	21.243	20.624	20.030	19.461	18.914	24
25	22.719	22.023	21.357	20.720	20.109	19.524	25
26	23.542	22.795	22.081	21.399	20.746	20.121	26
27	24.360	23.560	22.796	22.068	21.372	20.707	27
28	25.171	24.316	23.503	22.727	21.987	21.281	28
29	25.976	25.066	24.200	23.376	22.592	21.844	29
30	26.775	25.808	24.889	24.016	23.186	22.397	30
31	27.568	26.542	25.569	24.646	23.770	22.938	31
32	28.356	27.270	26.241	25.267	24.344	23.468	32
33	29.137	27.990	26.905	25.879	24.908	23.989	33
34	29.913	28.703	27.561	26.482	25.462	24.499	34
35	30.683	29.409	28.208	27.076	26.007	24.999	35
36	31.447	30.108	28.847	27.661	26.543	25.489	36
37	32.205	30.800	29.479	28.237	27.069	25.970	37
38	32.958	31.485	30.103	28.805	27.586	26.441	38
39	33.705	32.163	30.719	29.365	28.095	26.903	39
40	34.447	32.835	31.327	29.916	28.594	27.356	40
41	35.183	33.500	31.928	30.459	29.085	27.800	41
42	35.914	34.158	32.521	30.994	29.568	28.235	42
43	36.639	34.810	33.108	31.521	30.042	28.662	43
44	37.359	35.456	33.686	32.041	30.508	29.080	44
45	38.073	36.095	34.258	32.552	30.966	29.490	45
46	38.782	36.727	34.823	33.057	31.417	29.892	46
47	39.486	37.354	35.381	33.553	31.859	30.287	47
48	40.185	37.974	35.932	34.043	32.294	30.673	48
49	40.878	38.588	36.476	34.525	32.721	31.052	49
50	41.567	39.196	37.013	35.000	33.141	31.424	50

n	2½%	3%	3½%	4%	4½%	5%	n
1	0.976	0.971	0.966	0.962	0.957	0.952	1
2	1.927	1.914	1.900	1.886	1.873	1.859	2
3	2.856	2.829	2.802	2.775	2.749	2.723	3
4	3.762	3.717	3.673	3.630	3.588	3.546	4
5	4.646	4.580	4.515	4.452	4.390	4.330	5
6	5.508	5.417	5.329	5.242	5.158	5.076	6
7	6.349	6.230	6.115	6.002	5.893	5.786	7
8	7.170	7.020	6.874	6.733	6.596	6.463	8
9	7.971	7.786	7.608	7.435	7.269	7.108	9
10	8.752	8.530	8.317	8.111	7.913	7.722	10
11	9.514	9.253	9.002	8.761	8.529	8.306	11
12	10.258	9.954	9.663	9.385	9.119	8.863	12
13	10.983	10.635	10.303	9.986	9.683	9.394	13
14	11.691	11.296	10.921	10.563	10.223	9.899	14
15	12.381	11.938	11.517	11.118	10.740	10.380	15
16	13.055	12.561	12.094	11.652	11.234	10.838	16
17	13.712	13.166	12.651	12.166	11.707	11.274	17
18	14.353	13.754	13.190	12.659	12.160	11.690	18
19	14.979	14.324	13.710	13.134	12.593	12.085	19
20	15.589	14.878	14.212	13.590	13.008	12.462	20
21	16.185	15.415	14.698	14.029	13.405	12.821	21
22	16.765	15.937	15.167	14.451	13.784	13.163	22
23	17.332	16.444	15.620	14.857	14.148	13.489	23
24	17.885	16.936	16.058	15.247	14.496	13.799	24
25	18.424	17.413	16.482	15.622	14.828	14.094	25
26	18.951	17.877	16.890	15.983	15.147	14.375	26
27	19.464	18.327	17.285	16.330	15.451	14.643	27
28	19.965	18.764	17.667	16.663	15.743	14.898	28
29	20.454	19.189	18.036	16.984	16.022	15.141	29
30	20.930	19.600	18.392	17.292	16.289	15.373	30
31	21.395	20.000	18.736	17.589	16.544	15.593	31
32	21.849	20.389	19.069	17.874	16.789	15.803	32
33	22.292	20.766	19.390	18.148	17.023	16.003	33
34	22.724	21.132	19.701	18.411	17.247	16.193	34
35	23.145	21.487	20.001	18.665	17.461	16.374	35
36	23.556	21.832	20.291	18.908	17.666	16.547	36
37	23.957	22.167	20.571	19.143	17.862	16.711	37
38	24.349	22.493	20.841	19.368	18.050	16.868	38
39	24.730	22.808	21.103	19.585	18.230	17.017	39
40	25.103	23.115	21.355	19.793	18.402	17.159	40
41	25.466	23.412	21.599	19.993	18.566	17.294	41
42	25.821	23.701	21.835	20.186	18.724	17.423	42
43	26.167	23.982	22.063	20.371	18.874	17.546	43
44	26.504	24.254	22.283	20.549	19.018	17.663	44
45	26.833	24.519	22.496	20.720	19.156	17.774	45
46	27.154	24.776	22.701	20.885	19.288	17.880	46
47	27.468	25.025	22.899	21.043	19.415	17.981	47
48	27.773	25.167	23.091	21.195	19.536	18.077	48
49	28.071	25.502	23.277	21.342	19.651	18.169	49
50	28.362	25.730	23.456	21.482	19.762	18.256	50

n	5½%	6%	6½%	7%	7½%	8%	n
1	0.948	0.943	0.939	0.935	0.930	0.926	1
2	1.846	1.833	1.821	1.808	1.796	1.783	2
3	2.698	2.673	2.649	2.624	2.601	2.577	3
4	3.505	3.465	3.426	3.387	3.349	3.312	4
5	4.270	4.212	4.156	4.100	4.046	3.993	5
6	4.996	4.917	4.841	4.767	4.694	4.623	6
7	5.683	5.582	5.485	5.389	5.297	5.206	7
8	6.335	6.210	6.089	5.971	5.857	5.747	8
9	6.952	6.802	6.656	6.515	6.379	6.247	9
10	7.538	7.360	7.189	7.024	6.864	6.710	10
11	8.093	7.887	7.689	7.499	7.315	7.139	11
12	8.619	8.384	8.159	7.943	7.735	7.536	12
13	9.117	8.853	8.600	8.358	8.126	7.904	13
14	9.590	9.295	9.014	8.746	8.489	8.244	14
15	10.038	9.712	9.403	9.108	8.827	8.560	15
16	10.462	10.106	9.768	9.447	9.142	8.851	16
17	10.865	10.477	10.111	9.763	9.434	9.122	17
18	11.246	10.828	10.433	10.059	9.706	9.372	18
19	11.608	11.158	10.735	10.336	9.959	9.604	19
20	11.950	11.470	11.019	10.594	10.195	9.818	20
21	12.275	11.764	11.285	10.836	10.414	10.017	21
22	12.583	12.042	11.535	11.061	10.617	10.201	22
23	12.875	12.303	11.770	11.272	10.807	10.371	23
24	13.152	12.550	11.991	11.469	10.983	10.529	24
25	13.414	12.783	12.198	11.654	11.147	10.675	25
26	13.663	13.003	12.392	11.826	11.300	10.810	26
27	13.898	13.211	12.575	11.987	11.441	10.935	27
28	14.121	13.406	12.747	12.137	11.573	11.051	28
29	14.333	13.591	12.908	12.278	11.696	11.158	29
30	14.534	13.765	13.059	12.409	11.810	11.258	30
31	14.724	13.929	13.201	12.532	11.917	11.350	31
32	14.904	14.084	13.334	12.647	12.016	11.435	32
33	15.075	14.230	13.459	12.754	12.107	11.514	33
34	15.237	14.368	13.577	12.854	12.193	11.587	34
35	15.391	14.498	13.687	12.948	12.273	11.655	35
36	15.536	14.621	13.791	13.035	12.347	11.717	36
37	15.674	14.737	13.888	13.117	12.415	11.775	37
38	15.805	14.846	13.979	13.194	12.479	11.829	38
39	15.929	14.949	14.065	13.265	12.539	11.879	39
40	16.046	15.046	14.146	13.332	12.594	11.925	40
41	16.158	15.138	14.221	13.394	12.646	11.967	41
42	16.263	15.225	14.292	13.453	12.694	12.007	42
43	16.363	15.306	14.359	13.507	12.739	12.043	43
44	16.458	15.383	14.421	13.558	12.780	12.077	44
45	16.548	15.456	14.480	13.606	12.819	12.108	45
46	16.633	15.524	14.535	13.650	12.855	12.137	46
47	16.714	15.589	14.587	13.692	12.888	12.164	47
48	16.790	15.650	14.636	13.731	12.919	12.189	48
49	16.863	15.708	14.682	13.767	12.948	12.212	49
50	16.932	15.762	14.725	13.801	12.975	12.234	50

n	9%	10%	11%	12%	13%	14%	n
1	0.917	0.909	0.901	0.893	0.885	0.877	1
2	1.759	1.736	1.713	1.690	1.668	1.647	2
3	2.531	2.487	2.444	2.402	2.361	2.322	3
4	3.240	3.170	3.103	3.037	2.975	2.914	4
5	3.890	3.791	3.696	3.605	3.517	3.433	5
6	4.486	4.355	4.231	4.111	3.998	3.889	6
7	5.033	4.868	4.712	4.564	4.423	4.288	7
8	5.535	5.335	5.146	4.968	4.799	4.639	8
9	5.995	5.759	5.537	5.328	5.132	4.946	9
10	6.418	6.145	5.889	5.650	5.426	5.216	10
11	6.805	6.495	6.207	5.938	5.687	5.453	11
12	7.161	6.814	6.492	6.194	5.918	5.660	12
13	7.487	7.103	6.750	6.424	6.122	5.842	13
14	7.786	7.367	6.982	6.628	6.303	6.002	14
15	8.061	7.606	7.191	6.811	6.462	6.142	15
16	8.313	7.824	7.379	6.974	6.604	6.265	16
17	8.544	8.022	7.549	7.120	6.729	6.373	17
18	8.756	8.201	7.702	7.250	6.840	6.467	18
19	8.950	8.365	7.839	7.366	6.938	6.550	19
20	9.129	8.514	7.963	7.469	7.025	6.623	20
21	9.292	8.649	8.075	7.562	7.102	6.687	21
22	9.442	8.772	8.176	7.645	7.170	6.743	22
23	9.580	8.883	8.266	7.718	7.230	6.792	23
24	9.707	8.985	8.348	7.784	7.283	6.835	24
25	9.823	9.077	8.422	7.843	7.330	6.873	25
26	9.929	9.161	8.488	7.896	7.372	6.906	26
27	10.027	9.237	8.548	7.943	7.409	6.935	27
28	10.116	9.307	8.602	7.984	7.441	6.961	28
29	10.198	9.370	8.650	8.022	7.470	6.983	29
30	10.274	9.427	8.694	8.055	7.496	7.003	30
31	10.343	9.479	8.733	8.085	7.518	7.020	31
32	10.406	9.526	8.769	8.112	7.538	7.035	32
33	10.464	9.569	8.801	8.135	7.556	7.048	33
34	10.518	9.609	8.829	8.157	7.572	7.060	34
35	10.567	9.644	8.855	8.176	7.586	7.070	35
36	10.612	9.677	8.879	8.192	7.598	7.079	36
37	10.653	9.706	8.900	8.208	7.609	7.087	37
38	10.691	9.733	8.919	8.221	7.618	7.094	38
39	10.726	9.757	8.936	8.233	7.627	7.100	39
40	10.757	9.779	8.951	8.244	7.634	7.105	40
41	10.787	9.799	8.965	8.253	7.641	7.110	41
42	10.813	9.817	8.977	8.262	7.647	7.114	42
43	10.838	9.834	8.989	8.270	7.652	7.117	43
44	10.861	9.849	8.999	8.276	7.657	7.121	44
45	10.881	9.863	9.008	8.283	7.661	7.123	45
46	10.900	9.875	9.016	8.288	7.665	7.126	46
47	10.918	9.887	9.024	8.293	7.668	7.128	47
48	10.934	9.897	9.030	8.297	7.671	7.130	48
49	10.948	9.906	9.036	8.301	7.673	7.131	49
50	10.962	9.915	9.042	8.305	7.675	7.133	50

n	15%	16%	17%	18%	19%	20%	n
1	0.870	0.862	0.855	0.848	0.840	0.833	1
2	1.626	1.605	1.585	1.566	1.547	1.528	2
3	2.283	2.246	2.210	2.174	2.140	2.107	3
4	2.855	2.798	2.743	2.690	2.639	2.589	4
5	3.352	3.274	3.199	3.127	3.058	2.991	5
6	3.785	3.685	3.589	3.498	3.410	3.326	6
7	4.160	4.039	3.922	3.812	3.706	3.605	7
8	4.487	4.344	4.207	4.078	3.954	3.837	8
9	4.772	4.607	4.451	4.303	4.163	4.031	9
10	5.019	4.833	4.659	4.494	4.339	4.193	10
11	5.234	5.029	4.836	4.656	4.487	4.327	11
12	5.421	5.197	4.988	4.793	4.611	4.439	12
13	5.583	5.342	5.118	4.910	4.715	4.533	13
14	5.725	5.468	5.229	5.008	4.802	4.611	14
15	5.847	5.576	5.324	5.092	4.876	4.676	15
16	5.954	5.669	5.405	5.162	4.938	4.730	16
17	6.047	5.749	5.475	5.222	4.990	4.775	17
18	6.128	5.818	5.534	5.273	5.033	4.812	18
19	6.198	5.878	5.585	5.316	5.070	4.844	19
20	6.259	5.929	5.628	5.353	5.101	4.870	20
21	6.313	5.973	5.665	5.384	5.127	4.891	21
22	6.399	6.011	5.696	5.410	5.149	4.909	22
23	6.359	6.044	5.723	5.432	5.167	4.925	23
24	6.434	6.073	5.747	5.451	5.182	4.937	24
25	6.464	6.097	5.766	5.467	5.195	4.948	25
26	6.491	6.118	5.783	5.480	5.206	4.956	26
27	6.514	6.136	5.798	5.492	5.215	4.964	27
28	6.534	6.152	5.810	5.502	5.223	4.970	28
29	6.551	6.166	5.820	5.510	5.229	4.975	29
30	6.566	6.177	5.829	5.517	5.235	4.979	30
31	6.579	6.187	5.837	5.523	5.239	4.983	31
32	6.591	6.196	5.844	5.528	5.243	4.985	32
33	6.601	6.203	5.849	5.532	5.246	4.988	33
34	6.609	6.210	5.854	5.536	5.249	4.990	34
35	6.617	6.215	5.858	5.539	5.251	4.992	35
36	6.623	6.220	5.862	5.541	5.253	4.993	36
37	6.629	6.224	5.865	5.543	5.255	4.994	37
38	6.634	6.228	5.867	5.545	5.256	4.995	38
39	6.638	6.231	5.870	5.547	5.257	4.996	39
40	6.642	6.234	5.871	5.548	5.258	4.997	40
41	6.645	6.236	5.873	5.549	5.259	4.997	41
42	6.648	6.238	5.874	5.550	5.260	4.998	42
43	6.650	6.239	5.876	5.551	5.260	4.998	43
44	6.652	6.241	5.877	5.552	5.261	4.998	44
45	6.654	6.242	5.877	5.552	5.261	4.999	45
46	6.656	6.243	5.878	5.553	5.261	4.999	46
47	6.657	6.244	5.879	5.553	5.262	4.999	47
48	6.659	6.245	5.879	5.554	5.262	4.999	48
49	6.660	6.246	5.880	5.554	5.262	4.999	49
50	6.661	6.246	5.880	5.554	5.262	5.000	50

TABLE 5: The Present Value of $1/12 To Be Received Monthly for N Years (The Present Value of $1 to Be Received or Spent Each Year on a Monthly Basis Starting Now): $PV_{am} = S_{am} \times n] i$

n	1%	2%	3%	4%	5%	6%	7%	n
1	0.990	0.980	0.971	0.961	0.951	0.942	0.933	1
2	1.970	1.941	1.912	1.884	1.856	1.829	1.802	2
3	2.941	2.883	2.826	2.771	2.717	2.665	2.613	3
4	3.902	3.806	3.713	3.624	3.536	3.452	3.370	4
5	4.853	4.711	4.574	4.443	4.316	4.193	4.075	5
6	5.795	5.598	5.410	5.230	5.057	4.892	4.733	6
7	6.727	6.467	6.221	5.986	5.762	5.549	5.347	7
8	7.650	7.320	7.007	6.712	6.433	6.169	5.919	8
9	8.564	8.155	7.771	7.410	7.071	6.752	6.452	9
10	9.469	8.974	8.512	8.081	7.678	7.302	6.950	10
11	10.365	9.777	9.231	8.726	8.256	7.820	7.414	11
12	11.252	10.563	9.929	9.345	8.806	8.307	7.847	12
13	12.130	11.335	10.607	9.940	9.328	8.767	8.250	13
14	12.999	12.091	11.264	10.512	9.826	9.199	8.627	14
15	13.860	12.832	11.902	11.061	10.299	9.607	8.978	15
16	14.712	13.558	12.521	11.589	10.749	9.991	9.305	16
17	15.556	14.270	13.122	12.096	11.177	10.352	9.610	17
18	16.391	14.968	13.705	12.583	11.584	10.693	9.895	18
19	17.218	15.652	14.271	13.052	11.972	11.013	10.160	19
20	18.037	16.322	14.820	13.502	12.340	11.315	10.408	20
21	18.848	16.980	15.353	13.934	12.691	11.600	10.639	21
22	19.651	17.624	15.871	14.349	13.025	11.868	10.854	22
23	20.445	18.256	16.373	14.748	13.342	12.120	11.055	23
24	21.232	18.875	16.860	15.132	13.644	12.358	11.242	24
25	22.011	19.481	17.333	15.500	13.931	12.582	11.417	25
26	22.782	20.076	17.792	15.854	14.205	12.793	11.580	26
27	23.545	20.659	18.237	16.195	14.465	12.992	11.732	27
28	24.301	21.231	18.669	16.522	14.712	13.179	11.874	28
29	25.050	21.791	19.089	16.836	14.947	13.355	12.006	29
30	25.790	22.340	19.496	17.137	15.171	13.521	12.129	30
31	26.524	22.878	19.891	17.427	15.384	13.678	12.244	31
32	27.250	23.406	20.274	17.706	15.586	13.825	12.351	32
33	27.969	23.923	20.646	17.974	15.779	13.964	12.451	33
34	28.681	24.430	21.007	18.231	15.963	14.094	12.544	34
35	29.386	24.927	21.357	18.478	16.137	14.218	12.631	35
36	30.084	25.414	21.697	18.716	16.303	14.333	12.712	36
37	30.775	25.891	22.027	18.944	16.461	14.443	12.788	37
38	31.459	26.359	22.348	19.163	16.611	14.546	12.858	38
39	32.136	26.818	22.659	19.374	16.754	14.642	12.924	39
40	32.806	27.267	22.960	19.576	16.890	14.734	12.985	40
41	33.470	27.708	23.253	19.771	17.019	14.820	13.042	41
42	34.127	28.140	23.537	19.958	17.142	14.901	13.096	42
43	34.778	28.564	23.813	20.137	17.259	14.977	13.145	43
44	35.422	28.979	24.080	20.310	17.370	15.049	13.192	44
45	36.060	29.385	24.340	20.476	17.476	15.116	13.235	45
46	36.691	29.784	24.592	20.635	17.577	15.180	13.275	46
47	37.316	30.175	24.837	20.788	17.673	15.240	13.313	47
48	37.935	30.558	25.074	20.935	17.764	15.297	13.348	48
49	38.548	30.934	25.304	21.076	17.851	15.350	13.381	49
50	39.154	31.302	25.528	21.212	17.933	15.400	13.411	50

n	8%	9%	10%	11%	12%	13%	14%	n
1	0.923	0.914	0.905	0.896	0.888	0.879	0.870	1
2	1.776	1.750	1.725	1.700	1.675	1.651	1.627	2
3	2.563	2.514	2.466	2.420	2.374	2.329	2.286	3
4	3.290	3.213	3.138	3.065	2.994	2.926	2.859	4
5	3.961	3.852	3.746	3.643	3.545	3.449	3.357	5
6	4.581	4.436	4.296	4.162	4.033	3.910	3.791	6
7	5.153	4.969	4.794	4.626	4.467	4.314	4.169	7
8	5.682	5.457	5.245	5.043	4.851	4.670	4.497	8
9	6.170	5.904	5.653	5.416	5.193	4.982	4.783	9
10	6.620	6.312	6.022	5.751	5.496	5.256	5.031	10
11	7.036	6.685	6.357	6.051	5.765	5.498	5.248	11
12	7.420	7.025	6.659	6.319	6.003	5.710	5.436	12
13	7.775	7.337	6.933	6.560	6.215	5.896	5.600	13
14	8.103	7.622	7.181	6.776	6.403	6.059	5.742	14
15	8.405	7.883	7.406	6.970	6.570	6.203	5.866	15
16	8.684	8.121	7.609	7.143	6.718	6.329	5.974	16
17	8.942	8.339	7.793	7.298	6.849	6.440	6.068	17
18	9.180	8.538	7.960	7.438	6.966	6.538	6.149	18
19	9.400	8.720	8.110	7.563	7.069	6.624	6.220	19
20	9.603	8.886	8.247	7.675	7.161	6.699	6.282	20
21	9.790	9.038	8.370	7.775	7.243	6.765	6.336	21
22	9.963	9.177	8.482	7.865	7.315	6.823	6.383	22
23	10.123	9.305	8.583	7.945	7.379	6.875	6.424	23
24	10.271	9.421	8.675	8.018	7.436	6.919	6.459	24
25	10.407	9.527	8.758	8.082	7.486	6.959	6.490	25
26	10.533	9.624	8.833	8.140	7.531	6.994	6.517	26
27	10.649	9.713	8.901	8.192	7.571	7.024	6.540	27
28	10.756	9.794	8.962	8.239	7.606	7.051	6.560	28
29	10.855	9.869	9.018	8.281	7.638	7.074	6.578	29
30	10.947	9.937	9.069	8.318	7.666	7.095	6.593	30
31	11.031	9.999	9.114	8.352	7.690	7.113	6.607	31
32	11.109	10.055	9.155	8.382	7.712	7.129	6.618	32
33	11.181	10.107	9.193	8.409	7.732	7.143	6.628	33
34	11.247	10.155	9.227	8.433	7.749	7.155	6.637	34
35	11.309	10.198	9.257	8.455	7.764	7.166	6.645	35
36	11.365	10.238	9.285	8.474	7.778	7.176	6.651	36
37	11.418	10.274	9.310	8.491	7.790	7.184	6.657	37
38	11.466	10.307	9.333	8.507	7.801	7.191	6.662	38
39	11.511	10.337	9.354	8.521	7.810	7.198	6.667	39
40	11.552	10.365	9.372	8.533	7.818	7.204	6.671	40
41	11.590	10.390	9.389	8.545	7.826	7.209	6.674	41
42	11.625	10.414	9.404	8.555	7.833	7.213	6.677	42
43	11.658	10.435	9.418	8.564	7.838	7.217	6.679	43
44	11.688	10.454	9.431	8.572	7.844	7.220	6.681	44
45	11.715	10.472	9.442	8.579	7.848	7.223	6.683	45
46	11.741	10.488	9.452	8.586	7.852	7.226	6.685	46
47	11.764	10.503	9.461	8.591	7.856	7.228	6.686	47
48	11.786	10.516	9.470	8.597	7.859	7.230	6.688	48
49	11.806	10.529	9.477	8.601	7.862	7.232	6.689	49
50	11.825	10.540	9.484	8.605	7.865	7.233	6.690	50

n	15%	16%	17%	18%	19%	20%	n
1	0.862	0.853	0.845	0.836	0.828	0.820	1
2	1.604	1.581	1.558	1.536	1.514	1.493	2
3	2.243	2.202	2.161	2.121	2.082	2.044	3
4	2.794	2.731	2.670	2.610	2.553	2.497	4
5	3.269	3.183	3.100	3.020	2.942	2.867	5
6	3.677	3.568	3.463	3.362	3.265	3.172	6
7	4.030	3.897	3.770	3.648	3.532	3.421	7
8	4.333	4.177	4.029	3.888	3.754	3.626	8
9	4.595	4.416	4.248	4.088	3.937	3.793	9
10	4.820	4.620	4.433	4.256	4.089	3.931	10
11	5.014	4.794	4.589	4.396	4.214	4.044	11
12	5.181	4.943	4.721	4.513	4.319	4.136	12
13	5.325	5.070	4.832	4.611	4.405	4.212	13
14	5.449	5.178	4.926	4.693	4.476	4.274	14
15	5.556	5.270	5.006	4.762	4.535	4.326	15
16	5.648	5.348	5.073	4.819	4.584	4.367	16
17	5.727	5.416	5.130	4.867	4.625	4.402	17
18	5.796	5.473	5.178	4.907	4.659	4.430	18
19	5.854	5.522	5.218	4.941	4.686	4.453	19
20	5.905	5.563	5.252	4.969	4.709	4.472	20
21	5.949	5.599	5.281	4.992	4.728	4.487	21
22	5.987	5.629	5.305	5.012	4.744	4.500	22
23	6.019	5.655	5.326	5.028	4.757	4.511	23
24	6.047	5.677	5.343	5.042	4.768	4.519	24
25	6.071	5.696	5.358	5.053	4.777	4.526	25
26	6.092	5.712	5.371	5.063	4.785	4.532	26
27	6.110	5.725	5.381	5.071	4.791	4.537	27
28	6.125	5.737	5.390	5.078	4.796	4.540	28
29	6.138	5.747	5.397	5.083	4.800	4.544	29
30	6.150	5.756	5.404	5.088	4.804	4.546	30
31	6.160	5.763	5.409	5.092	4.807	4.548	31
32	6.168	5.769	5.414	5.095	4.809	4.550	32
33	6.175	5.774	5.417	5.098	4.811	4.552	33
34	6.182	5.779	5.421	5.100	4.813	4.553	34
35	6.187	5.783	5.423	5.102	4.814	4.554	35
36	6.192	5.786	5.426	5.104	4.815	4.555	36
37	6.196	5.789	5.427	5.105	4.816	4.555	37
38	6.199	5.791	5.429	5.106	4.817	4.556	38
39	6.202	5.793	5.431	5.107	4.817	4.556	39
40	6.205	5.795	5.432	5.108	4.818	4.556	40
41	6.207	5.796	5.433	5.109	4.818	4.557	41
42	6.209	5.798	5.434	5.109	4.819	4.557	42
43	6.210	5.799	5.434	5.110	4.819	4.557	43
44	6.212	5.800	5.435	5.110	4.819	4.557	44
45	6.213	5.800	5.435	5.110	4.819	4.558	45
46	6.214	5.801	5.436	5.111	4.820	4.558	46
47	6.215	5.802	5.436	5.111	4.820	4.558	47
48	6.216	5.802	5.436	5.111	4.820	4.558	48
49	6.217	5.802	5.437	5.111	4.820	4.558	49
50	6.217	5.803	5.437	5.111	4.820	4.558	50

TABLE 6: The Present Value of $1/12 To Be Received Monthly in Year *N* (The Present Value of Annual Sums of $1 to Be Received or Spent Monthly During Some Year in the Future): $PV_{am} = S_{am} \times n]\,i$

n	1%	2%	3%	4%	5%	6%	7%	n
1	0.990	0.980	0.971	0.961	0.951	0.942	0.933	1
2	0.980	0.961	0.942	0.923	0.905	0.887	0.870	2
3	0.971	0.942	0.914	0.887	0.861	0.836	0.811	3
4	0.961	0.923	0.887	0.852	0.819	0.787	0.756	4
5	0.951	0.905	0.861	0.819	0.779	0.741	0.705	5
6	0.942	0.887	0.836	0.787	0.741	0.698	0.658	6
7	0.932	0.870	0.811	0.756	0.705	0.658	0.614	7
8	0.923	0.852	0.787	0.727	0.671	0.620	0.572	8
9	0.914	0.835	0.764	0.698	0.638	0.584	0.534	9
10	0.905	0.819	0.741	0.671	0.607	0.550	0.498	10
11	0.896	0.803	0.719	0.645	0.578	0.518	0.464	11
12	0.887	0.787	0.698	0.619	0.550	0.488	0.433	12
13	0.878	0.771	0.677	0.595	0.523	0.459	0.404	13
14	0.869	0.756	0.657	0.572	0.497	0.433	0.376	14
15	0.861	0.741	0.638	0.549	0.473	0.408	0.351	15
16	0.852	0.726	0.619	0.528	0.450	0.384	0.327	16
17	0.844	0.712	0.601	0.507	0.428	0.362	0.305	17
18	0.835	0.698	0.583	0.487	0.407	0.341	0.285	18
19	0.827	0.684	0.566	0.468	0.388	0.321	0.266	19
20	0.819	0.671	0.549	0.450	0.369	0.302	0.248	20
21	0.811	0.657	0.533	0.432	0.351	0.285	0.231	21
22	0.803	0.644	0.517	0.415	0.334	0.268	0.215	22
23	0.795	0.632	0.502	0.399	0.317	0.253	0.201	23
24	0.787	0.619	0.487	0.384	0.302	0.238	0.187	24
25	0.779	0.607	0.473	0.369	0.287	0.224	0.175	25
26	0.771	0.595	0.459	0.354	0.273	0.211	0.163	26
27	0.764	0.583	0.445	0.340	0.260	0.199	0.152	27
28	0.756	0.572	0.432	0.327	0.247	0.187	0.142	28
29	0.748	0.560	0.419	0.314	0.235	0.176	0.132	29
30	0.741	0.549	0.407	0.302	0.224	0.166	0.123	30
31	0.734	0.538	0.395	0.290	0.213	0.156	0.115	31
32	0.726	0.528	0.383	0.279	0.203	0.147	0.107	32
33	0.719	0.517	0.372	0.268	0.193	0.139	0.100	33
34	0.712	0.507	0.361	0.257	0.183	0.131	0.093	34
35	0.705	0.497	0.350	0.247	0.174	0.123	0.087	35
36	0.698	0.487	0.340	0.238	0.166	0.116	0.081	36
37	0.691	0.477	0.330	0.228	0.158	0.109	0.076	37
38	0.684	0.468	0.320	0.219	0.150	0.103	0.071	38
39	0.677	0.459	0.311	0.211	0.143	0.097	0.066	39
40	0.670	0.450	0.302	0.202	0.136	0.091	0.061	40
41	0.664	0.441	0.293	0.195	0.129	0.086	0.057	41
42	0.657	0.432	0.284	0.187	0.123	0.081	0.053	42
43	0.651	0.424	0.276	0.180	0.117	0.076	0.050	43
44	0.644	0.415	0.268	0.173	0.111	0.072	0.046	44
45	0.638	0.407	0.260	0.166	0.106	0.068	0.043	45
46	0.631	0.399	0.252	0.159	0.101	0.064	0.040	46
47	0.625	0.391	0.245	0.153	0.096	0.060	0.038	47
48	0.619	0.383	0.237	0.147	0.091	0.057	0.035	48
49	0.613	0.376	0.230	0.141	0.087	0.053	0.033	49
50	0.607	0.368	0.224	0.136	0.083	0.050	0.031	50

n	8%	9%	10%	11%	12%	13%	14%	n
1	0.923	0.914	0.905	0.896	0.888	0.879	0.870	1
2	0.853	0.836	0.819	0.803	0.788	0.772	0.757	2
3	0.787	0.764	0.742	0.720	0.699	0.679	0.659	3
4	0.727	0.699	0.671	0.645	0.620	0.596	0.573	4
5	0.671	0.639	0.608	0.578	0.551	0.524	0.499	5
6	0.620	0.584	0.550	0.518	0.489	0.460	0.434	6
7	0.572	0.534	0.498	0.465	0.434	0.405	0.378	7
8	0.528	0.488	0.451	0.417	0.385	0.355	0.328	8
9	0.488	0.446	0.408	0.373	0.341	0.312	0.286	9
10	0.451	0.408	0.369	0.335	0.303	0.274	0.249	10
11	0.416	0.373	0.334	0.300	0.269	0.241	0.216	11
12	0.384	0.341	0.303	0.269	0.239	0.212	0.188	12
13	0.355	0.312	0.274	0.241	0.212	0.186	0.164	13
14	0.328	0.285	0.248	0.216	0.188	0.164	0.143	14
15	0.302	0.261	0.225	0.194	0.167	0.144	0.124	15
16	0.279	0.238	0.203	0.173	0.148	0.126	0.108	16
17	0.258	0.218	0.184	0.155	0.131	0.111	0.094	17
18	0.238	0.199	0.167	0.139	0.117	0.098	0.082	18
19	0.220	0.182	0.151	0.125	0.104	0.086	0.071	19
20	0.203	0.166	0.137	0.112	0.092	0.075	0.062	20
21	0.187	0.152	0.124	0.100	0.082	0.066	0.054	21
22	0.173	0.139	0.112	0.090	0.072	0.058	0.047	22
23	0.160	0.127	0.101	0.081	0.064	0.051	0.041	23
24	0.148	0.116	0.092	0.072	0.057	0.045	0.035	24
25	0.136	0.106	0.083	0.065	0.051	0.040	0.031	25
26	0.126	0.097	0.075	0.058	0.045	0.035	0.027	26
27	0.116	0.089	0.068	0.052	0.040	0.031	0.023	27
28	0.107	0.081	0.062	0.047	0.035	0.027	0.020	28
29	0.099	0.074	0.056	0.042	0.031	0.024	0.018	29
30	0.091	0.068	0.050	0.037	0.028	0.021	0.015	30
31	0.084	0.062	0.046	0.034	0.025	0.018	0.013	31
32	0.078	0.057	0.041	0.030	0.022	0.016	0.012	32
33	0.072	0.052	0.037	0.027	0.019	0.014	0.010	33
34	0.067	0.047	0.034	0.024	0.017	0.012	0.009	34
35	0.061	0.043	0.031	0.022	0.015	0.011	0.008	35
36	0.057	0.040	0.028	0.019	0.014	0.010	0.007	36
37	0.052	0.036	0.025	0.017	0.012	0.008	0.006	37
38	0.048	0.033	0.023	0.016	0.011	0.007	0.005	38
39	0.045	0.030	0.021	0.014	0.010	0.007	0.004	39
40	0.041	0.028	0.019	0.013	0.008	0.006	0.004	40
41	0.038	0.025	0.017	0.011	0.008	0.005	0.003	41
42	0.035	0.023	0.015	0.010	0.007	0.004	0.003	42
43	0.032	0.021	0.014	0.009	0.006	0.004	0.003	43
44	0.030	0.019	0.013	0.008	0.005	0.003	0.002	44
45	0.028	0.018	0.011	0.007	0.005	0.003	0.002	45
46	0.026	0.016	0.010	0.007	0.004	0.003	0.002	46
47	0.024	0.015	0.009	0.006	0.004	0.002	0.001	47
48	0.022	0.014	0.008	0.005	0.003	0.002	0.001	48
49	0.020	0.012	0.008	0.005	0.003	0.002	0.001	49
50	0.019	0.011	0.007	0.004	0.003	0.002	0.001	50

n	15%	16%	17%	18%	19%	20%	n
1	0.862	0.853	0.845	0.836	0.828	0.820	1
2	0.742	0.728	0.714	0.700	0.686	0.673	2
3	0.639	0.621	0.603	0.585	0.568	0.552	3
4	0.551	0.530	0.509	0.489	0.471	0.452	4
5	0.475	0.452	0.430	0.409	0.390	0.371	5
6	0.409	0.385	0.363	0.342	0.323	0.304	6
7	0.352	0.329	0.307	0.286	0.267	0.250	7
8	0.303	0.280	0.259	0.240	0.221	0.205	8
9	0.261	0.239	0.219	0.200	0.183	0.168	9
10	0.225	0.204	0.185	0.168	0.152	0.138	10
11	0.194	0.174	0.156	0.140	0.126	0.113	11
12	0.167	0.149	0.132	0.117	0.104	0.093	12
13	0.144	0.127	0.111	0.098	0.086	0.076	13
14	0.124	0.108	0.094	0.082	0.071	0.062	14
15	0.107	0.092	0.080	0.069	0.059	0.051	15
16	0.092	0.079	0.067	0.057	0.049	0.042	16
17	0.079	0.067	0.057	0.048	0.041	0.034	17
18	0.068	0.057	0.048	0.040	0.034	0.028	18
19	0.059	0.049	0.041	0.034	0.028	0.023	19
20	0.051	0.042	0.034	0.028	0.023	0.019	20
21	0.044	0.036	0.029	0.024	0.019	0.016	21
22	0.038	0.030	0.024	0.020	0.016	0.013	22
23	0.032	0.026	0.021	0.016	0.013	0.010	23
24	0.028	0.022	0.017	0.014	0.011	0.009	24
25	0.024	0.019	0.015	0.012	0.009	0.007	25
26	0.021	0.016	0.012	0.010	0.007	0.006	26
27	0.018	0.014	0.011	0.008	0.006	0.005	27
28	0.015	0.012	0.009	0.007	0.005	0.004	28
29	0.013	0.010	0.008	0.006	0.004	0.003	29
30	0.011	0.009	0.006	0.005	0.004	0.003	30
31	0.010	0.007	0.005	0.004	0.003	0.002	31
32	0.009	0.006	0.005	0.003	0.002	0.002	32
33	0.007	0.005	0.004	0.003	0.002	0.001	33
34	0.006	0.005	0.003	0.002	0.002	0.001	34
35	0.005	0.004	0.003	0.002	0.001	0.001	35
36	0.005	0.003	0.002	0.002	0.001	0.001	36
37	0.004	0.003	0.002	0.001	0.001	0.001	37
38	0.004	0.002	0.002	0.001	0.001	0.001	38
39	0.003	0.002	0.001	0.001	0.001	0.000	39
40	0.003	0.002	0.001	0.001	0.001	0.000	40
41	0.002	0.002	0.001	0.001	0.000	0.000	41
42	0.002	0.001	0.001	0.001	0.000	0.000	42
43	0.002	0.001	0.001	0.001	0.000	0.000	43
44	0.001	0.001	0.001	0.000	0.000	0.000	44
45	0.001	0.001	0.001	0.000	0.000	0.000	45
46	0.001	0.001	0.000	0.000	0.000	0.000	46
47	0.001	0.001	0.000	0.000	0.000	0.000	47
48	0.001	0.001	0.000	0.000	0.000	0.000	48
49	0.001	0.000	0.000	0.000	0.000	0.000	49
50	0.001	0.000	0.000	0.000	0.000	0.000	50

TABLE 7: The Present Value of the Depreciation of $1 Utilizing The Double-Declining-Balance Method

n	1%	2%	3%	4%	5%	6%	7%	n
1								1
2								2
3	0.986	0.972	0.958	0.945	0.933	0.920	0.908	3
4	0.982	0.964	0.947	0.930	0.914	0.898	0.883	4
5	0.978	0.956	0.936	0.916	0.897	0.878	0.860	5
6	0.974	0.948	0.924	0.901	0.879	0.858	0.838	6
7	0.970	0.941	0.914	0.888	0.863	0.840	0.817	7
8	0.966	0.934	0.903	0.874	0.847	0.822	0.797	8
9	0.962	0.926	0.893	0.862	0.832	0.804	0.778	9
10	0.958	0.919	0.883	0.849	0.817	0.787	0.759	10
11	0.954	0.912	0.873	0.836	0.803	0.771	0.742	11
12	0.951	0.905	0.863	0.824	0.788	0.755	0.724	12
13	0.947	0.898	0.854	0.813	0.775	0.740	0.708	13
14	0.943	0.891	0.844	0.801	0.762	0.725	0.692	14
15	0.939	0.885	0.835	0.790	0.749	0.711	0.677	15
16	0.936	0.878	0.826	0.779	0.736	0.697	0.662	16
17	0.932	0.871	0.817	0.768	0.724	0.684	0.648	17
18	0.928	0.865	0.808	0.757	0.712	0.671	0.634	18
19	0.925	0.858	0.800	0.747	0.701	0.659	0.621	19
20	0.921	0.852	0.791	0.737	0.689	0.647	0.609	20
21	0.918	0.846	0.783	0.727	0.678	0.635	0.596	21
22	0.914	0.839	0.775	0.718	0.668	0.624	0.584	22
23	0.911	0.833	0.767	0.708	0.657	0.613	0.573	23
24	0.907	0.827	0.759	0.699	0.647	0.602	0.562	24
25	0.904	0.821	0.751	0.690	0.638	0.592	0.551	25
26	0.900	0.815	0.743	0.681	0.628	0.582	0.541	26
27	0.897	0.810	0.736	0.673	0.619	0.572	0.531	27
28	0.893	0.804	0.728	0.664	0.610	0.562	0.522	28
29	0.890	0.798	0.721	0.656	0.601	0.553	0.512	29
30	0.886	0.792	0.714	0.648	0.592	0.544	0.503	30
31	0.883	0.787	0.707	0.640	0.584	0.536	0.495	31
32	0.880	0.781	0.700	0.632	0.575	0.527	0.486	32
33	0.876	0.776	0.693	0.625	0.568	0.519	0.478	33
34	0.873	0.770	0.687	0.617	0.560	0.511	0.470	34
35	0.870	0.765	0.680	0.610	0.552	0.503	0.462	35
36	0.867	0.760	0.673	0.603	0.545	0.496	0.455	36
37	0.863	0.755	0.667	0.596	0.537	0.489	0.448	37
38	0.860	0.749	0.661	0.589	0.530	0.482	0.441	38
39	0.857	0.744	0.655	0.582	0.523	0.475	0.434	39
40	0.854	0.739	0.649	0.576	0.517	0.468	0.427	40
41	0.850	0.734	0.643	0.569	0.510	0.461	0.421	41
42	0.847	0.729	0.637	0.563	0.504	0.455	0.415	42
43	0.844	0.724	0.631	0.557	0.497	0.449	0.409	43
44	0.841	0.720	0.625	0.551	0.491	0.443	0.403	44
45	0.838	0.715	0.620	0.545	0.485	0.437	0.397	45
46	0.835	0.710	0.614	0.539	0.479	0.431	0.391	46
47	0.832	0.706	0.609	0.533	0.474	0.425	0.386	47
48	0.829	0.701	0.603	0.528	0.468	0.420	0.381	48
49	0.826	0.696	0.598	0.522	0.463	0.415	0.376	49
50	0.823	0.692	0.593	0.517	0.457	0.409	0.370	50

n	8%	9%	10%	11%	12%	13%	14%	n
1								1
2								2
3	0.896	0.885	0.873	0.862	0.852	0.841	0.831	3
4	0.868	0.854	0.841	0.827	0.814	0.802	0.789	4
5	0.843	0.827	0.811	0.796	0.781	0.767	0.753	5
6	0.819	0.800	0.783	0.766	0.749	0.733	0.718	6
7	0.796	0.776	0.756	0.738	0.720	0.703	0.687	7
8	0.774	0.752	0.731	0.711	0.693	0.675	0.657	8
9	0.753	0.730	0.708	0.687	0.667	0.648	0.631	9
10	0.733	0.709	0.685	0.663	0.643	0.623	0.605	10
11	0.714	0.688	0.664	0.642	0.620	0.600	0.582	11
12	0.696	0.669	0.644	0.621	0.599	0.579	0.559	12
13	0.678	0.651	0.625	0.601	0.579	0.558	0.539	13
14	0.661	0.633	0.607	0.583	0.560	0.539	0.520	14
15	0.645	0.617	0.590	0.565	0.543	0.521	0.502	15
16	0.630	0.600	0.573	0.549	0.526	0.504	0.485	16
17	0.615	0.585	0.558	0.533	0.510	0.489	0.469	17
18	0.601	0.571	0.543	0.518	0.495	0.473	0.454	18
19	0.587	0.557	0.529	0.504	0.481	0.459	0.440	19
20	0.574	0.543	0.515	0.490	0.467	0.446	0.427	20
21	0.562	0.531	0.503	0.477	0.454	0.433	0.414	21
22	0.550	0.518	0.490	0.465	0.442	0.421	0.402	22
23	0.538	0.507	0.479	0.453	0.431	0.410	0.391	23
24	0.527	0.495	0.467	0.442	0.420	0.399	0.380	24
25	0.516	0.485	0.457	0.432	0.409	0.389	0.370	25
26	0.506	0.474	0.446	0.421	0.399	0.379	0.361	26
27	0.496	0.464	0.436	0.412	0.390	0.370	0.352	27
28	0.486	0.455	0.427	0.402	0.380	0.361	0.343	28
29	0.477	0.445	0.418	0.394	0.372	0.352	0.335	29
30	0.468	0.436	0.409	0.385	0.363	0.344	0.327	30
31	0.459	0.428	0.401	0.377	0.356	0.337	0.319	31
32	0.451	0.420	0.393	0.369	0.348	0.329	0.312	32
33	0.442	0.412	0.385	0.362	0.341	0.322	0.306	33
34	0.435	0.404	0.378	0.354	0.334	0.315	0.299	34
35	0.427	0.397	0.370	0.347	0.327	0.309	0.293	35
36	0.420	0.390	0.364	0.341	0.321	0.303	0.287	36
37	0.413	0.383	0.357	0.334	0.314	0.297	0.281	37
38	0.406	0.376	0.350	0.328	0.308	0.291	0.275	38
39	0.399	0.370	0.344	0.322	0.303	0.285	0.270	39
40	0.393	0.364	0.338	0.316	0.297	0.280	0.265	40
41	0.387	0.358	0.333	0.311	0.292	0.275	0.260	41
42	0.381	0.352	0.327	0.305	0.287	0.270	0.255	42
43	0.375	0.346	0.322	0.300	0.282	0.265	0.251	43
44	0.369	0.341	0.316	0.295	0.277	0.261	0.246	44
45	0.364	0.335	0.311	0.290	0.272	0.256	0.242	45
46	0.358	0.330	0.306	0.286	0.268	0.252	0.238	46
47	0.353	0.325	0.302	0.281	0.264	0.248	0.234	47
48	0.348	0.321	0.297	0.277	0.259	0.244	0.230	48
49	0.343	0.316	0.293	0.273	0.255	0.240	0.227	49
50	0.338	0.311	0.288	0.269	0.251	0.236	0.223	50

n	15%	16%	17%	18%	19%	20%	n
1							1
2							2
3	0.821	0.811	0.802	0.792	0.783	0.774	3
4	0.778	0.766	0.755	0.744	0.733	0.723	4
5	0.739	0.727	0.714	0.702	0.690	0.679	5
6	0.704	0.690	0.676	0.663	0.650	0.638	6
7	0.671	0.657	0.642	0.628	0.615	0.603	7
8	0.641	0.626	0.611	0.596	0.583	0.570	8
9	0.614	0.597	0.582	0.567	0.554	0.540	9
10	0.588	0.571	0.555	0.541	0.526	0.513	10
11	0.564	0.547	0.531	0.516	0.502	0.488	11
12	0.541	0.525	0.509	0.493	0.479	0.466	12
13	0.521	0.504	0.488	0.473	0.459	0.445	13
14	0.501	0.484	0.468	0.453	0.439	0.426	14
15	0.484	0.466	0.451	0.436	0.422	0.409	15
16	0.467	0.450	0.434	0.419	0.405	0.392	16
17	0.451	0.434	0.418	0.404	0.390	0.377	17
18	0.436	0.419	0.404	0.389	0.376	0.363	18
19	0.422	0.405	0.390	0.376	0.363	0.350	19
20	0.409	0.392	0.377	0.363	0.350	0.338	20
21	0.397	0.380	0.365	0.352	0.339	0.327	21
22	0.385	0.369	0.354	0.341	0.328	0.316	22
23	0.374	0.358	0.344	0.330	0.318	0.306	23
24	0.363	0.348	0.334	0.321	0.308	0.297	24
25	0.354	0.338	0.324	0.311	0.299	0.288	25
26	0.344	0.329	0.315	0.303	0.291	0.280	26
27	0.335	0.320	0.307	0.294	0.283	0.272	27
28	0.327	0.312	0.299	0.287	0.275	0.265	28
29	0.319	0.305	0.291	0.279	0.268	0.258	29
30	0.311	0.297	0.284	0.272	0.262	0.251	30
31	0.304	0.290	0.277	0.266	0.255	0.245	31
32	0.297	0.283	0.271	0.259	0.249	0.239	32
33	0.290	0.277	0.265	0.253	0.243	0.234	33
34	0.284	0.271	0.259	0.248	0.238	0.228	34
35	0.278	0.265	0.253	0.242	0.232	0.223	35
36	0.272	0.259	0.248	0.237	0.227	0.218	36
37	0.267	0.254	0.242	0.232	0.222	0.213	37
38	0.261	0.249	0.238	0.227	0.218	0.209	38
39	0.256	0.244	0.233	0.223	0.213	0.205	39
40	0.251	0.239	0.228	0.218	0.209	0.200	40
41	0.247	0.235	0.224	0.214	0.205	0.196	41
42	0.242	0.230	0.220	0.210	0.201	0.193	42
43	0.238	0.226	0.215	0.206	0.197	0.189	43
44	0.234	0.222	0.212	0.202	0.193	0.185	44
45	0.229	0.218	0.208	0.198	0.190	0.182	45
46	0.226	0.214	0.204	0.195	0.187	0.179	46
47	0.222	0.211	0.201	0.192	0.183	0.176	47
48	0.218	0.207	0.197	0.188	0.180	0.173	48
49	0.215	0.204	0.194	0.185	0.177	0.170	49
50	0.211	0.200	0.191	0.182	0.174	0.167	50

TABLE 8: The Present Value of the Depreciation of $1 Utilizing The Sum-Of-The-Years'-Digits Method (Where the Salvage Value Is Under 10%)

n	1%	2%	3%	4%	5%	6%	7%	n
1								1
2								2
3	0.984	0.968	0.952	0.937	0.923	0.908	0.895	3
4	0.980	0.961	0.943	0.925	0.908	0.892	0.875	4
5	0.977	0.955	0.934	0.914	0.894	0.875	0.857	5
6	0.974	0.949	0.925	0.902	0.880	0.859	0.839	6
7	0.971	0.943	0.916	0.891	0.867	0.844	0.822	7
8	0.968	0.937	0.908	0.880	0.854	0.829	0.805	8
9	0.964	0.931	0.899	0.869	0.841	0.814	0.789	9
10	0.961	0.925	0.891	0.859	0.829	0.800	0.773	10
11	0.958	0.919	0.883	0.848	0.816	0.786	0.758	11
12	0.955	0.913	0.874	0.838	0.804	0.773	0.743	12
13	0.952	0.908	0.866	0.828	0.793	0.760	0.729	13
14	0.949	0.902	0.858	0.818	0.781	0.747	0.715	14
15	0.946	0.896	0.851	0.809	0.770	0.734	0.701	15
16	0.943	0.891	0.843	0.799	0.759	0.722	0.688	16
17	0.940	0.885	0.835	0.790	0.749	0.711	0.676	17
18	0.937	0.880	0.828	0.781	0.738	0.699	0.663	18
19	0.934	0.874	0.820	0.772	0.728	0.688	0.652	19
20	0.931	0.869	0.813	0.763	0.718	0.677	0.640	20
21	0.928	0.863	0.806	0.754	0.708	0.666	0.629	21
22	0.925	0.858	0.799	0.746	0.699	0.656	0.618	22
23	0.922	0.853	0.792	0.738	0.689	0.646	0.607	23
24	0.919	0.848	0.785	0.729	0.680	0.636	0.597	24
25	0.916	0.843	0.778	0.721	0.671	0.627	0.587	25
26	0.913	0.838	0.771	0.714	0.662	0.617	0.577	26
27	0.910	0.832	0.765	0.706	0.654	0.608	0.567	27
28	0.907	0.827	0.758	0.698	0.645	0.599	0.558	28
29	0.904	0.823	0.752	0.691	0.637	0.590	0.549	29
30	0.902	0.818	0.746	0.683	0.629	0.582	0.540	30
31	0.899	0.813	0.739	0.676	0.621	0.574	0.532	31
32	0.896	0.808	0.733	0.669	0.614	0.566	0.524	32
33	0.893	0.803	0.727	0.662	0.606	0.558	0.516	33
34	0.890	0.798	0.721	0.655	0.599	0.550	0.508	34
35	0.888	0.794	0.715	0.648	0.591	0.542	0.500	35
36	0.885	0.789	0.709	0.642	0.584	0.535	0.493	36
37	0.882	0.785	0.703	0.635	0.577	0.528	0.485	37
38	0.879	0.780	0.698	0.629	0.570	0.521	0.478	38
39	0.877	0.776	0.692	0.622	0.564	0.514	0.471	39
40	0.874	0.771	0.686	0.616	0.557	0.507	0.465	40
41	0.871	0.767	0.681	0.610	0.551	0.501	0.458	41
42	0.868	0.762	0.676	0.604	0.544	0.494	0.452	42
43	0.866	0.758	0.670	0.598	0.538	0.488	0.445	43
44	0.863	0.754	0.665	0.592	0.532	0.482	0.439	44
45	0.860	0.749	0.660	0.587	0.526	0.476	0.433	45
46	0.858	0.745	0.655	0.581	0.520	0.470	0.428	46
47	0.855	0.741	0.649	0.575	0.515	0.464	0.422	47
48	0.853	0.737	0.644	0.570	0.509	0.459	0.416	48
49	0.850	0.733	0.639	0.565	0.503	0.453	0.411	49
50	0.847	0.729	0.635	0.559	0.498	0.448	0.406	50

n	8%	9%	10%	11%	12%	13%	14%	n
1								1
2								2
3	0.881	0.868	0.855	0.843	0.831	0.819	0.808	3
4	0.860	0.845	0.830	0.816	0.802	0.789	0.776	4
5	0.839	0.822	0.806	0.790	0.775	0.760	0.746	5
6	0.820	0.801	0.783	0.766	0.749	0.734	0.718	6
7	0.801	0.781	0.761	0.743	0.725	0.708	0.692	7
8	0.782	0.761	0.740	0.721	0.702	0.684	0.667	8
9	0.765	0.742	0.720	0.700	0.680	0.661	0.643	9
10	0.748	0.724	0.701	0.680	0.659	0.640	0.621	10
11	0.732	0.706	0.683	0.660	0.639	0.619	0.600	11
12	0.715	0.689	0.665	0.642	0.620	0.600	0.581	12
13	0.700	0.673	0.648	0.624	0.602	0.581	0.562	13
14	0.685	0.658	0.632	0.608	0.585	0.564	0.544	14
15	0.671	0.643	0.616	0.592	0.569	0.547	0.527	15
16	0.657	0.628	0.601	0.576	0.553	0.532	0.511	16
17	0.644	0.614	0.587	0.562	0.538	0.516	0.496	17
18	0.631	0.601	0.573	0.548	0.524	0.502	0.482	18
19	0.618	0.588	0.560	0.534	0.510	0.488	0.468	19
20	0.606	0.575	0.547	0.521	0.497	0.475	0.455	20
21	0.594	0.563	0.535	0.509	0.485	0.463	0.443	21
22	0.583	0.552	0.523	0.497	0.473	0.451	0.431	22
23	0.572	0.540	0.512	0.485	0.461	0.440	0.420	23
24	0.561	0.529	0.501	0.474	0.450	0.429	0.409	24
25	0.551	0.519	0.490	0.464	0.440	0.418	0.398	25
26	0.541	0.509	0.480	0.454	0.430	0.408	0.389	26
27	0.531	0.499	0.470	0.444	0.420	0.399	0.379	27
28	0.522	0.489	0.460	0.434	0.411	0.390	0.370	28
29	0.513	0.480	0.451	0.425	0.402	0.381	0.362	29
30	0.504	0.471	0.442	0.417	0.393	0.372	0.353	30
31	0.495	0.463	0.434	0.408	0.385	0.364	0.345	31
32	0.487	0.454	0.426	0.400	0.377	0.356	0.338	32
33	0.479	0.446	0.418	0.392	0.369	0.349	0.330	33
34	0.471	0.439	0.410	0.385	0.362	0.342	0.323	34
35	0.463	0.431	0.403	0.377	0.355	0.335	0.317	35
36	0.456	0.424	0.395	0.370	0.348	0.328	0.310	36
37	0.449	0.416	0.388	0.363	0.341	0.322	0.304	37
38	0.442	0.410	0.382	0.357	0.335	0.315	0.298	38
39	0.435	0.403	0.375	0.350	0.329	0.309	0.292	39
40	0.428	0.396	0.369	0.344	0.323	0.304	0.287	40
41	0.422	0.390	0.362	0.338	0.317	0.298	0.281	41
42	0.415	0.384	0.356	0.333	0.311	0.293	0.276	42
43	0.409	0.378	0.351	0.327	0.306	0.287	0.271	43
44	0.403	0.372	0.345	0.321	0.301	0.282	0.266	44
45	0.397	0.366	0.340	0.316	0.296	0.278	0.261	45
46	0.392	0.361	0.334	0.311	0.291	0.273	0.257	46
47	0.386	0.355	0.329	0.306	0.286	0.268	0.253	47
48	0.381	0.350	0.324	0.301	0.281	0.264	0.248	48
49	0.375	0.345	0.319	0.297	0.277	0.260	0.244	49
50	0.370	0.340	0.314	0.292	0.273	0.255	0.240	50

n	15%	16%	17%	18%	19%	20%	n
1							1
2							2
3	0.796	0.786	0.775	0.765	0.755	0.745	3
4	0.763	0.751	0.739	0.728	0.717	0.706	4
5	0.732	0.719	0.706	0.694	0.682	0.670	5
6	0.703	0.689	0.675	0.662	0.649	0.637	6
7	0.676	0.661	0.647	0.633	0.619	0.606	7
8	0.651	0.635	0.620	0.605	0.592	0.578	8
9	0.626	0.610	0.595	0.580	0.566	0.552	9
10	0.604	0.587	0.571	0.556	0.542	0.528	10
11	0.583	0.566	0.549	0.534	0.519	0.506	11
12	0.562	0.545	0.529	0.513	0.499	0.485	12
13	0.543	0.526	0.510	0.494	0.479	0.465	13
14	0.525	0.508	0.491	0.476	0.461	0.447	14
15	0.509	0.491	0.474	0.459	0.444	0.430	15
16	0.492	0.475	0.458	0.443	0.428	0.414	16
17	0.477	0.460	0.443	0.428	0.413	0.400	17
18	0.463	0.445	0.429	0.414	0.399	0.386	18
19	0.449	0.432	0.415	0.400	0.386	0.373	19
20	0.436	0.419	0.403	0.388	0.373	0.360	20
21	0.424	0.407	0.391	0.376	0.362	0.349	21
22	0.412	0.395	0.379	0.364	0.351	0.338	22
23	0.401	0.384	0.368	0.354	0.340	0.328	23
24	0.390	0.374	0.358	0.344	0.330	0.318	24
25	0.380	0.364	0.348	0.334	0.321	0.309	25
26	0.371	0.354	0.339	0.325	0.312	0.300	26
27	0.361	0.345	0.330	0.316	0.303	0.292	27
28	0.353	0.336	0.322	0.308	0.295	0.284	28
29	0.344	0.328	0.314	0.300	0.288	0.276	29
30	0.336	0.320	0.306	0.293	0.280	0.269	30
31	0.328	0.313	0.298	0.285	0.273	0.262	31
32	0.321	0.306	0.291	0.279	0.267	0.256	32
33	0.314	0.299	0.285	0.272	0.260	0.250	33
34	0.307	0.292	0.278	0.266	0.254	0.244	34
35	0.300	0.286	0.272	0.260	0.249	0.238	35
36	0.294	0.280	0.266	0.254	0.243	0.233	36
37	0.288	0.274	0.261	0.249	0.238	0.228	37
38	0.282	0.268	0.255	0.243	0.233	0.223	38
39	0.277	0.263	0.250	0.238	0.228	0.218	39
40	0.271	0.257	0.245	0.233	0.223	0.213	40
41	0.266	0.252	0.240	0.229	0.219	0.209	41
42	0.261	0.248	0.235	0.224	0.214	0.205	42
43	0.256	0.243	0.231	0.220	0.210	0.201	43
44	0.252	0.238	0.227	0.216	0.206	0.197	44
45	0.247	0.234	0.222	0.212	0.202	0.193	45
46	0.243	0.230	0.218	0.208	0.198	0.190	46
47	0.238	0.226	0.214	0.204	0.195	0.186	47
48	0.234	0.222	0.211	0.201	0.191	0.183	48
49	0.230	0.218	0.207	0.197	0.188	0.180	49
50	0.227	0.215	0.204	0.194	0.185	0.177	50

Glossary of Terms

A

ACCRUAL, ACCRUALS, ACCRUED: Costs that were incurred, although not paid, during a particular period.

ACID TEST: A measure of a firm's liquidity using the formula (Current Assets − Inventories)/Current Liabilities. Also called the *quick ratio*.

ACCOUNTING RATE OF RETURN: A method of capital budgeting that employs the percentage of gain from the annual income of a project in relation to the amount of capital investment. It is expressed as the reciprocal of the *payback period*. (See also Payback Period.)

ACCOUNTS RECEIVABLE: Those sums outstanding as a result of sales, and hence, after losses for uncollectible accounts have been deducted, part of the current assets of the firm.

AMORTIZATION: Provision for the periodic retirement of a company's long-term debts, generally bonds, over a period of years prior to their maturity through either early redemption or the establishment of a sinking fund.

ANNUALIZING: The process of ranking projects of different economic lives for purposes of comparison, which is accomplished by dividing the net total present value profits of each by the appropriate present value factor of an annuity of $1.

ANNUITY: An amount payable or receivable at regular intervals. (See also Tax-Sheltered Annuity.)

APPLICATION OF FUNDS: Part of the *statement of the source and application of funds*. Basically this refers to increases in assets and decreases in liabilities and stockholders' equity. Also called *use of funds*. (See also Source of Funds and Statement of the Source and Application of Funds.)

ASSETS: All resources belonging to a company, including those of both short-term and long-term duration.

AT: Abbreviation for "after-tax."

AVERAGE COLLECTION PERIOD: The number of days that accounts receivable are outstanding.

B

BALANCE SHEET: See Financial Position Statement.

BANK INTEREST: That form of discount loan in which the total interest is deducted from the principal in advance.

BASIS POINT: A change of .01% in the yield of a security. Therefore, 100 basis points = 1%.

BOND: A long-term instrument of debt, or *promissory note*, whose pledge of repayment is secured by the issuing agency.

BOOK-VALUE: Those amounts cited in connection with items listed in a company's financial position statement. Also used to express the value of a share of the firm's common stock based upon these figures.

BT: Abbreviation for "before-tax."

C

CAPITAL BUDGETING: The process by which a company allocates funds to particular projects or uses.

CAPITAL GAIN: A profit earned by selling long- or short-term assets. With the sale of long-term assets, a different rate of federal income tax prevails.

CAPITAL, PAID-IN: See Surplus.

CAPITAL RATIONING: Restrictions that a firm may place upon the use of the comparatively limited amount of funds available to it.

CAPITAL STRUCTURE: The composition of the firm's capitalization as it relates to long-term debt, preferred stock, and common stock (common stockholders' equity). (See also Capitalization.)

CAPITAL SURPLUS: See Surplus.

CAPITALIZATION: The total capital structure of a firm, including long-term debt, preferred stock, and common stock (common stockholders' equity). Also, the process of determining the value of a company by dividing its average historic earnings by an appropriate discount rate.

CASH FLOW: The result of the after-tax net inflows and outflows of cash items in the operations of a firm. This is an important component of funds flow, and one in which cash is one form of capital involved. (See also Flow of Working Capital and Funds Flow.)

CLOSED-END MUTUAL FUND: See Mutual Fund and Open-End Mutual Fund.

COLLECTION PERIOD: See Average Collection Period.

COMMON-SIZE ANALYSIS: The process of reducing all items in the financial position and income statements to a percentage of total assets or sales, respectively.

COMMON STOCK: The shares of securities that compose the ownership of a corporation. (See also Common Stockholders' Equity.)

COMMON STOCKHOLDERS' EQUITY: Those equity funds, such as paid-in capital and retained income, possessed by the corporation but constituting part of the value of shares owned by the common stockholders. (See also Common Stock.)

COMPENSATING BALANCE: The sum of money that a firm must keep on deposit at no interest with the bank that lends it funds, generally around 20% of the amount of the loan outstanding.

COMPOUND INTEREST: Interest accruing to both the principal and to the interest that has already been accumulated.

CONVERTIBLE BOND: A bond that can be exchanged, usually for a company's common stock, at some fixed ratio of conversion.

COST OF CAPITAL: The percentage amount that a firm must pay for its capital. (See also the Weighted Cost of Capital.)

COUPON RATE: The stated rate of interest that a bond declares it will pay.

CUMULATIVE DIVIDENDS: Dividends with preferred stock that, if discontinued or "passed" by a corporation, accumulate and must be made up prior to the payment of any dividends to common stockholders. (See also Non-Cumulative Dividends.)

CURRENT ASSETS: Abbreviated to CA. A firm's resources that are readily convertible into cash within its normal operating period, usually a year.

CURRENT LIABILITIES: Abbreviated to CL. A firm's debts that are expected to be paid in full within its normal operating period, usually a year.

CURRENT RATIO: A measure of a firm's liquidity, expressed as Current Assets/Current Liabilities.

D

DEBENTURE: That form of bond that is not secured by a lien upon any specific property owned by the firm. (See also Subordinated Debenture.)

DEFERRED CHARGES: Costs that will ultimately be paid by a firm, but not within the current accounting period. Therefore, deferred charges are temporarily considered part of the company's assets.

DEPRECIATION: The estimated decrease in the value of a long-lived asset, computed annually for tax and accounting purposes. A variety of methods may be used to compute depreciation, including the straight-line, double-declining-balance, and sum-of-the-years'-digits methods.

DILUTION: The increase of the number of common shares beyond that proportionate growth of the firm's income necessary to keep the amount earned per share constant.

DISCOUNT RATE: A term usually referring to the percentage cost of the firm's capital and used in determining its present value calculations.

DISCOUNT TERMS: A percentage reduction in a bill paid early, generally appearing in a notation such as "2/10 n 30" or "2/10 net 30," meaning a 2% discount if the bill is paid by the tenth of the month. (See also EOM.)

DIVIDEND: An amount paid by the firm to a shareholder. The precise amount is specified only in the case of preferred stock. (See also Stock Dividend.)

DIVIDEND PAYOUT: The proportion of earnings AT per share paid as a dividend to the common stockholder, or Dividend per Share/Earnings AT per Share.

DIVIDEND YIELD: The relationship between the common stock dividend per share and cost per share, or Dividend per Share/Price per Share.

E

EBIT: Abbreviation for "earnings before interest and taxes."

EFFECTIVE RATE OF INTEREST: The actual rate of interest paid, in contrast to some stated rate. Also called *true interest.* (See also Coupon Rate.)

EOM: Abbreviation for "end of the month." Generally used with discount terms if both the discount and net periods commence after the end of the then-current month. (See also Discount Terms.)

EPS: Abbreviation for "earnings per share."

EQUITY: See Net Worth and Common Stockholders' Equity.

F

FACE VALUE: See Par.

FINANCIAL BREAK-EVEN POINT: That amount of earnings before interest and taxes (EBIT) needed so that the burden of different forms of capital do not dilute the firm's earnings. Also called the *indifference point.*

FINANCIAL POSITION STATE-MENT: A basic financial document that shows the balance between the firm's assets and its liabilities plus stockholders' equity at the end of a stated period, generally a year. Also called a *balance sheet.*

FIXED ASSETS: The firm's long-term resources that are regularly depreciated, such as plant and equipment.

FLOW OF WORKING CAPITAL: The result of changes in the inflows and outflows of a firm's cash and "near-cash" items. This constitutes an important element in funds flow. (See also Cash Flow, Funds Flow, and Working Capital.)

FUNDS FLOW: The end product of all after-tax net inflows and outflows of the firm's capital after the company's non-cash expenditures, such as depreciation and amortization, have been added back. (See also Cash Flow, and Flow of Working Capital.)

G

GOOD WILL: The premium recorded on the books of a company as an intangible asset whenever payment for that asset—usually a firm that has been purchased—exceeds its book value.

GROSS MARGIN: The amount remaining when the cost of goods sold is deducted from sales.

GROWTH RATE: The rate, generally compounded, at which a firm's earnings per share have been increasing.

H

HURDLE RATE: The rate of return, expressed in the form of a percentage, that the firm feels it must exceed in order to undertake a particular project.

I

INCOME STATEMENT: A basic financial document showing the gain or loss achieved by the firm during a stated period, generally a year. Also called a *profit and loss statement.*

INCREMENTAL ANALYSIS: Measuring a series of projects by starting with the one requiring the least investment and measuring it against the others by comparing their incremental outflows and inflows.

INDIFFERENCE POINT: See Financial Break-Even Point.

INITIAL OUTLAY: The expense that a firm expects to incur, or actually incurs, at the outset of a project.

INSTALLMENT PURCHASE: Buying an asset on the basis of regular payments per period that include capital repayment, interest, and frequently other charges as well.

INTEREST: See Compound Interest, EBIT, Effective Rate of Interest,

Merchant's Rule (For Interest), United States Rule (For Interest).

INTERNAL RATE OF RETURN: A method of evaluating a project by equalizing the present values of the cash inflows and outflows after determining the appropriate discount rate. Also called the *yield on investment method*.

INTERPOLATION: The means by which the precise internal rate of return is computed once the general percentages it lies between have been determined. (See also Internal Rate of Return.)

INVESTMENT RETIREMENT ACCOUNT: A tax-shelter that enables employed individuals not covered by any other retirement plan to invest a percentage of their income and to defer payment of income tax on this sum. Abbreviated to IRA.

IRA: Abbreviation for "investment retirement account."

K

KEOGH PLAN: A tax-shelter that enables certain self-employed individuals to invest a percentage of their income and to defer payment of income tax on this sum.

L

LEVERAGE: The use of fixed-charged debt in place of common equity capital with the objective of enhancing the firm's earnings for the common stockholder. Leverage occurs whenever the earnings rate exceeds the rate for the cost of the debt capital.

LIQUIDITY: The measure of a firm's capacity for quickly converting its assets into cash.

LOAD MUTUAL FUND: A mutual fund that, in addition to the usual fees paid to management, charges a fixed percentage on every sale of new shares. (See also Mutual Fund.)

M

MANAGEMENT OF FUNDS: The measure of a firm's ability to use its resources effectively, particularly its current assets.

MARGIN OF SAFETY: An estimate, generally expressed in the form of a percentage, of the risk factors existing in the operation of a company. Also called *risk factor*. (See also Risk.)

MERCHANT'S RULE (FOR INTEREST): A formula for computing the interest on the original debt and each succeeding partial payment up to the due date of the loan.

MERGER: The acquisition of one firm by another, resulting in the combining of their earnings, assets, and liabilities, including stockholders' equity.

MUNICIPALS: Bonds that are issued by local and state governmental agencies and whose interest is not counted as taxable income by the federal government. Some bonds may be exempt from state and/or local income taxes as well.

MUTUAL FUND: A managed investment fund that holds securities of various kinds. Such funds may be of different types, such as "load" or "no-load," and "open-end" or "closed-end." (See Load Mutual Fund and Open-End Mutual Fund.)

N

NAT: Abbreviation for "net after tax."

NET CURRENT ASSETS: See Working Capital.

NET PRESENT VALUE INDEX: A measure for ranking various projects by using the net present value method. It involves dividing the present value of the cash inflows by that of the cash outflows. Also called *profitability index*. (See also Present Value.)

NET PRESENT VALUE METHOD: A method of evaluating a project by computing the present values of the cash inflows less those of its cash outflows, all discounted at a given rate. A positive value suggests the acceptability of the project. (See also Present Value.)

NET WORKING CAPITAL: See Working Capital.

NET WORTH: Total stockholders' equity, both preferred and common. This is the same as total assets minus total liabilities.

NI: Abbreviation for "net income," which includes non-operating income, as distinguished from net operating income. (See also NOI.)

NOI: Abbreviation for "net operating income." Net operating income is distinct from net income, which includes non-operating income as well. (See also NI.)

NO-LOAD MUTUAL FUND: See Load Mutual Fund and Mutual Fund.

NON-CUMULATIVE DIVIDENDS: Dividends from preferred stock that the corporation may pass (that is, not pay) and that need never be made up. (See also Cumulative Dividends.)

NOTES RECEIVABLE: Debts owed to a firm and secured by signed notes.

O

OPEN-END MUTUAL FUND: A mutual fund that places no limit on the number of shares that it may issue, in contrast to a closed-end fund, which may issue only a specified number of shares. (See also Mutual Fund.)

OPPORTUNITY COST OF CAPITAL: The amount, expressed as a percentage, that the firm could earn by investing its capital elsewhere.

P

PAID-IN CAPITAL: See Common Stock.

PAR: The amount that is listed upon a security as its "nominal value." Also called *face value*.

PAYBACK PERIOD: A method of capital budgeting that is based on the time required for the cash flow AT from a project to regain the firm's initial outlay of capital. (See also Accounting Rate of Return.)

PAYOUT RATIO: See Dividend Payout.

PE RATIO: Abbreviation for "price-earnings ratio," which measures the relation between the price and earnings AT of a firm's common stock.

PPS: Abbreviation for "price per share" of common stock.

PREEMPTIVE RIGHTS: See Rights.

PREPAID EXPENSES: The cost of services for which the firm has already paid in advance of the current accounting period and which, therefore, is recorded in the financial position statement as a current asset.

PRESENT VALUE: The worth today of funds acquired or spent in the future when they are discounted over a specified period at a particular rate of compound interest. The result may be a single amount or a series of amounts paid over a given period of time. (See also Annuity.)

PROFIT AND LOSS STATEMENT: See Income Statement.

PROFITABILITY INDEX: See Net Present Value Index.

PRO FORMA: A hypothetical or anticipated statement of financial data presented in advance of the event.

PRO-RATE: To distribute over a period of time proportional amounts of expense or income that would more appropriately be charged to a variety of accounts rather than to just one.

Q

QUALITATIVE FACTORS: Those elements in a financial situation that must be assessed in a non-quantitive, non-mathematical fashion. (See also Quantitative Factors.)

QUANTITATIVE FACTORS: Those elements in a financial situation that lend themselves to solution by computational or mathematical means. (See also Qualitative Factors.)

QUICK RATIO: See Acid Test.

R

RESERVES: See Surplus.

RETAINED EARNINGS (INCOME): That portion of annual income AT, less dividends, that is held cumulatively by the corporation and is part of common stockholders' equity.

RIGHTS: A grant of permission, generally given to stockholders for a short period of time, to purchase a new issue of a firm's securities.

With common stock, the price is usually somewhat lower than that currently prevailing in the market. Also called *preemptive rights*. (See also Warrant.)

RISK: The dangers that a company may face, for example, diminished profitability, loss of income, capital losses, and even an end to its existence as a business entity. (See also Margin of Safety and Risk Factor.)

RISK FACTOR: The amount of added risk in an investment in a company's bonds, as compared to an investment in high-rated government securities. (See also Risk and Margin of Safety.)

ROI: Abbreviation for "rate of return on the firm's investment" (its total assets), and a measure of its profitability computed from Earnings AT/Total Assets.

ROIC: Abbreviation for "rate of return on invested capital." Also called *ROOI*. (See ROOI).

ROOI: Abbreviation for "rate of return on owners' investment," or the firm's net worth (which is the total of the preferred and common stockholders' equity.) This is a measure of a company's profitability. Also commonly called *ROIC*.

S

SINKING FUND: Annual sums that a firm generally sets aside from its income AT for the purpose of eventually redeeming its bonds or preferred stock.

SOURCE OF FUNDS: Part of the statement of the source and application of funds. Basically, "source of funds" refers to decreases in assets and increases in liabilities and stockholders' equity.

(See also Application of Funds and Statement of the Source and Application of Funds.)

STATEMENT OF THE SOURCE AND APPLICATION OF FUNDS: A basic financial document that presents the increases or decreases in the firm's assets and liabilities and stockholders' equity by reconciling the sources and uses of funds over a designated period, usually a year.

STOCK DIVIDEND: The payment of a dividend to common stockholders in the form of shares of additional stock instead of cash.

STOCKHOLDERS' EQUITY: See Net Worth and Common Stockholders' Equity.

STOCK SPLIT: The division of the outstanding common stock proportionate to the number of shares held by the existing common stockholders.

SUBORDINATED DEBENTURE: A debenture, or bond, that is not secured by any tangible assets of the company and whose claim for repayment is of a lower order than the firm's ordinary indebtedness or bonds that represent a mortgage or "lien" on the company. (See also Debenture.)

SURPLUS: Retained income that has been set aside for special purposes. Also called *reserves*.

T

TAX: Abbreviated to *t*. This generally refers to the federal tax rate. (See also Tax Shield.)

TAX ADJUSTMENT: The recalculation of a firm's income BT. It can be expressed as AT Amount of Income/$(1 - t)$.

TAX RELATED: See Tax Shield.

TAX SHELTER: An investment of income, and its accumulating gains, on which federal tax can be deferred. (See also Keogh Plan, Investment Retirement Account, and Tax-Sheltered Annuity.)

TAX-SHELTERED ANNUITY: The investment of income on a periodic basis, on which federal income tax may be deferred. (See Keogh Plan, Investment Retirement Account, and Tax Shelter.)

TAX SHIELD: This is the *tax related* $(1 - t)$, or actual, cost of any tax-deductible item to the firm. (See also Tax.)

TRADE DISCOUNT: See Discount Terms and EOM.

TREASURY STOCK: Shares of common stock reacquired by the company and deducted from its net worth in the financial position statement.

TRUE INTEREST: See Effective Rate of Interest.

U

UNITED STATES RULE (FOR INTEREST): Payment of a rate of interest based upon the amount of the remainder of principal due on the debt at the end of each payment period.

USE OF FUNDS: See Application of Funds and Statement of the Source and Application of Funds.

W

WARRANT: A right, granted for a considerable length of time, to purchase a specified number of a firm's common shares at some stated price. (See also Rights.)

WEIGHTED COST OF CAPITAL:
The firm's overall cost of capital when computed on the basis of the proportion of each type of capital times its cost AT.

WORKING CAPITAL: Current assets minus current liabilities, or CA − CL. Also called *net current assets*. This popularly serves to indicate the relative state of the various components of a firm's cash and near-cash items. (See also Current Assets, Current Liabilities, and Flow of Working Capital.)

Y

YIELD ON INVESTMENT METHOD: See Internal Rate of Return.

YIELD TO MATURITY: The rate of interest that a bond purchased at a certain price will yield from the receipt of both its interest payments and the return of its face-value principal if it is held to the date of maturity.

Index